Racing Shadows

IA Moore

Wild Horse Publishing
Copyright © 2023 by IA Moore
ISBN: 9798871679517

This book is a work of fiction. The characters, incidents, and dialogues are products of the author's imagination and are not to be construed as real. Any resemblance to actual persons, living or dead, is entirely coincidental.

All rights reserved. This book, or any portion thereof, may not be reproduced or used in any manner whatsoever without the express written permission of the author, except for the use of brief quotations in a book review.

ACKNOWLEDGMENTS

Special thanks to Myckie Neubauer, Thoroughbred Racehorse Trainer, for authentication of the horse racing details.

DEDICATIONS

This book is dedicated to racing fans and horse lovers everywhere.

Racing Shadows

CHAPTER 1

Shadow Adams pushed open the heavy doors of the hay room, squinting against the sunlight. She glanced down the shed row and observed the line of handsome heads hanging over their stall doors. Seeing the beautiful horses made her smile. Half of the thoroughbreds were up and either looking around at the world outside their stalls or lazily pulling hay from their nets. The others had probably gone back to bed for a nap. Satisfied that the morning's tasks were completed, she stepped onto one of the roads that connected the race track barns to one another.

The backside of the track lay quiet, seeming almost sleepy under the noon sun. So much different than the chaos of early morning. To one side, an elderly groom grazed a chestnut horse. A few people walked about casually as though they hadn't a care in the world. Shadow took a deep breath. She was relieved to have made it to Fort Eldon Race Track; in fact, almost happy.

She'd traveled over two thousand miles across country to get here, arriving early yesterday. She'd quickly secured a job and found a place to live. She was starting over—starting a new life. Was two thousand miles far enough, though, she wondered?

"Heading to the kitchen?"

Startled, she turned to see the speaker. It was Peter, the groom who had been assigned to showing her the ropes at her new job.

"Sorry. I didn't mean to scare you."

"Oh, hey. Not your fault. I was lost in thought and you surprised me," she replied. "Yes, I'm going to the kitchen. You?"

"That's exactly where I'm heading. I'm famished." He fell into step beside her.

As Shadow looked down at him, he turned his face up to her and gave her a smile. Her heart did a small involuntary flip: Peter the groom was the spitting image of Peter Dinklage the actor. When she'd first been introduced to him that morning, she had thought he *was* the real Peter Dinklage, especially with his name being literally … Peter! Maybe that was why she still felt a little star-struck by him even though she knew he wasn't an actual star. *Honestly, Shadow, get a grip,* she told herself. She had no time for silliness these days.

"Me too," she agreed.

"By the way, you did really well today."

"I did?" she asked, puzzled.

"With the horses. It was obvious that you've worked with racehorses before."

Racing Shadows

"Oh," she laughed, understanding what he meant. "Thanks so much. And yes, I've worked with racehorses before. Back ho—" she began to say, then corrected herself: this was her home now. "Back where I came from."

"Where's that?" he asked. The top of his head, which was covered with a knit black cap, fell well below her shoulder. And she wasn't overly tall. It didn't faze her though as she'd worked with jockeys for years and was entirely accustomed to their often diminutive size. Peter though was not diminutive: he was sturdy and gave out an aura of rugged strength.

"I'm from out west. Edmonton," she said.

"So you worked at Northlands?"

"Yes."

"Beautiful country out west."

"For sure!" Shadow's foster parents had taken her along on a trip to Jasper one year. She'd loved sitting in a hot spring while taking in a view of pine trees and snow-capped mountains.

They reached the kitchen. Shadow didn't particularly want to talk to anyone, not even someone who looked like a movie star. She had things to think about and her new life to figure out. The air fare here had eaten up her savings and payday wasn't until Friday. She had to be careful of her spending until then. At the same time, she couldn't afford to starve herself— not now.

She could think of no polite way of getting rid of Peter, so after picking up her food from the counter, she found herself sitting across from him at a small table facing a window.

She took a bite of her hotdog and a sip of chocolate milk as she snuck a glance at him. His eyes were a gorgeous soft green—she had to try hard not to fall into them. She felt herself flushing. Fortunately, he seemed to sense her disquiet and looked down, into his salad. She breathed a sigh of relief.

"Still eatin' that rabbit food, eh Pete," said a heavy man who pulled a third chair over to their table and plonked down his coffee and sandwich.

"You know me, Joe. Always watching my figure."

The man guffawed. "Right." Then a few seconds later: "How are you expecting the race to play out this afternoon?"

"Which one?"

"The filly allowance on the grass going six. I have one in there."

"Well, I expect my filly to win, of course," Peter said, grinning. His grin made Shadow's heart flutter and she looked away.

"Do you think it'll stay on the turf or come off?" asked Joe.

"Likely stay, but your guess is as good as mine. My horse is good either way."

As the men dissolved into banter about the day's race card, Shadow relaxed, relieved that nobody was paying her any attention. Occasionally she glanced up to sneak a peek at Peter. The resemblance to Peter Dinklage was uncanny. Could it possibly be that...? *No,*

Racing Shadows

of course not—what a stupid thought, she chided herself.

"This is Shadow," she heard Peter say. Realizing she was being addressed, she looked up. "And Shadow, this is Joe. Joe rubs horses a couple of barns over from us."

"Glad to meet ya," said Joe. "I haven't seen you 'round here before. You're new, aren't you?"

Shadow froze. The man was too large, too loud, too forward, too frightening.

"Shadow just started walking hots for us this morning." Peter said, saving her from replying. She gave him a quick smile, thanking him.

"Well, you're a right pretty one. You can come walk my hots anytime you want, girl!" Joe said, and then laughed.

Peter looked at her apologetically, shrugging one shoulder. He seemed to understand that Joe made her uncomfortable.

As Shadow stood up to leave, she sensed Peter's hand on her wrist, his touch so gentle she barely felt it. "Wait for me outside," he said. "I'll be out in a minute and I need to talk to you."

Shadow nodded. "Sure."

Then she dumped her trash, returned her tray, and walked out the door without looking back at the table. Much to her annoyance, she found herself trembling. Firstly, because she felt she'd embarrassed herself, reacting to simple joking by running away, and secondly, because the spot on her wrist where Peter had touched her was tingling.

She waited around the kitchen corner, leaning against the brick and letting the sun warm her face.

"Hey," said Peter as he walked out the door.

Shadow smiled at him. "I apologize. I cut your lunch short."

He smiled. "I was done. Me and Joe hash over the same stuff every day. No worries."

"I feel like it was rude of me to get up and leave so abruptly."

He chuckled and gave her a kind smile. "I must apologize for his commenting on your appearance and such. That's just the way trackers are. It's a condition without a cure."

She laughed. "Is he a friend of yours?"

Peter held up his hand, palm down, and tilted it side to side. "So-so. Joe likes to bet and he's always looking for inside information on the horses. Little does he know how poor my handicapping skills actually are."

"I'm just a little on edge—new place, new job and all." She wasn't about to explain the true reason for her nervousness to him … or to anybody. As if anyone would understand when sometimes she barely understood herself. "Did you want to talk to me about something?"

"Yes, I do. The boss has you down for cooling out the filly we were just talking about. I was wondering if you could take her to the paddock as well—Billie

Racing Shadows

Okayed it. I would but I've got one to get ready for the next race."

"Oh sure. Love to!" Shadow knew that afforded her a chance to earn some extra money.

"Great. She's a beauty. She won't give you too much trouble."

"Was she the grey walker from this morning?"

"Yes. She walked because she's racing today. Harold took her. I didn't know you'd noticed her."

"I love grey horses. And she's a real beauty. Huge for a filly, too."

"Yes. She's one of the barn favorites. And I'm pretty sure she'll win today."

"You're sure?"

"Well, it is a horse race and anything can happen, but…"

"And does," she laughed. She thought back to some of the wild things that had happened. "What's the craziest thing you've seen or heard of happening in a race?" she asked him as they began walking back to the barn.

He laughed. "So many options." He paused as though thinking. "There was the time that a horse lost its jockey during a race, simultaneously slamming into a second horse, and knocking the jockey of the second horse onto its back. So the jock finished the race on the wrong horse. That was hilarious. And luckily, nobody was hurt."

"Oh my goodness. He didn't win, did he?"

"No. He ended up finishing last. I can't imagine what would have happened had he won. I could see fans screaming bloody murder if the stewards disqualified him and they had bet money on him."

"Why would they disqualify him?" she asked, "if he had a jockey on him when he won?"

"I think the rule is that the horse must finish the race carrying the weight assigned him for the full distance of the race. So between the instant the assigned jockey fell off the horse and the instant the second jockey ended up on him, he would have been running without weight on his back which would disqualify him—even if it were a mere second or two. But I can see the fans objecting to the ruling if they had bet him!"

"Yes, sometimes they get pretty excited." She grinned. "I heard that once a dead jockey won a race. I believe that win was valid."

"I remember that. It was valid, yep. Technically, although the rider was no longer alive, the horse was still carrying his weight when he crossed the finish line."

"That must've been heartbreaking though," she said. "The owners must've been happy their horse won, but horrified that the jockey died riding it!"

"Yes. I surely would have been upset had it been my horse. The horse was named Sweet Kiss and I understand she never raced again. They called her 'The Sweet Kiss of Death' after that."

"Wow…. The horse I'm taking to the paddock today. Isn't her name Kiss?"

Racing Shadows

"Yes. Fortunately no relation—well, likely some relation as all thoroughbreds stem from the same three sires. But no close relation."

"Whew, good. What's her full name?"

"Kiss n' Tell. Something I'd never do by the way," he said, then rushed to add, "I mean ... I didn't mean anything by that ... honestly." Shadow looked down at him to see he was blushing.

Shadow began to laugh and doubled over trying to stop. She knew she was being impolite but couldn't help herself. "I'm sorry," she said when she caught her breath. "It's been a tough few days for me and I think I just finally relaxed!"

"That's good ... I guess," he said.

"I apologize. I really didn't mean to laugh. It was just that you looked so embarrassed."

"So you found it funny that I said I wouldn't kiss and tell because ... well, who would want to kiss me?"

"Of course not! Don't be silly. You're very attractive and I would ... I mean if the occasion arose ... I mean..." It was her turn to blush.

She heard him chuckle. "Now that we've cleared the air on that point, how about we get back to horses?"

"Perfect," she said, shaking her head at her gullibility, but giving him a smile.

Once back at the barn, Shadow stepped into the tack room where she'd left her jacket that morning. Peter waited outside.

"Well, bye," she said. "When should I be back here?"

"Two-thirty. See you then." He smiled as she turned to leave and she could sense him watching her walk away. It was stupid, but she felt as though he suspected....

She'd rented a room in a house on the street that ran along the far border of the race track. As she walked, she watched the people and horses still inside the compound, beyond the chain-link fence with its triple-stranded, barbed-wire top. Clearly, no one could reach them there. It made her envious. If only someone could have done that for her: put her behind barbed wire. If only...

The room is dark. And almost quiet. Except for the squeak of the bed, the rasp of sheets against flesh, the muffled sobs. Shadow watches the girl crying on the bed. Tears soak her embroidered pillowcase, so that one bright red flower sticks, sticks to the amber skin of her face. It seems as if the girl is in amber: a small creature caught in amber. Shadow wants to cry for the amber girl, but she can't.

Shadow commanded herself to stop slipping back into the past. *Get a grip!* she told herself. *It's over.* She squeezed her eyes shut and tried to concentrate on something else, something simple, and finally, she succeeded, forming an image of the new house in her

Racing Shadows

mind. Yes, the house where she would live now. Where she would begin her new life.

When she arrived, the shaggy dog that guarded the yard barked furiously. "Hi, Squeaks," she said, and that was all that it took for him to remember her. He quieted, wagging his tail. She walked up a narrow gravel driveway that bridged a deep weed-covered ditch. The plop of frogs jumping into the water and the manic chirping of crickets serenaded her, welcoming her back.

After climbing a short set of stairs, she entered her new home, one in which she hoped she'd be safe and— if even possible now—happy. Halfway down the narrow hall, she turned left and stepped over the threshold of her rented room. It contained a bed, dresser, night table, desk and chair, and a huge, empty bookcase. Beside the bed lay a gaudy, braided rug, the floor beneath it dark, polished wood. There was a lot of empty space and she wished the room were smaller. Because somehow she herself felt small, not quite grown up, and vulnerable to things she couldn't even name that might be hiding in such a large room.

Making the room seem even larger was the fact that the end wall was completely covered in mirrored tile streaked with a grey marbled pattern. In the center of the room lay her battered pink suitcase, still unopened on the gleaming floor. As she lifted and set it onto the bed for unpacking, she caught her own image in the wall, marbled with streaks of smokiness, indistinct. She looked like an abstract piece of art: an eye here, brown, a nose, a length of dark hair, the curve of a breast.

IA Moore

A rap on the door ... two ... three. *Who would be knocking?* she wondered as she approached the door, paused a second, turned the knob, and pulled it open. A stranger stood before her. His face was emotionless at first, then his lips curved up in a smile. "I wasn't sure you were in," he said.

Annoyed, she blurted, "I was told only women could rent here. What do you want?"

"I'm Mrs. Shevchuk's son, Paul Shevchuk." His face was smooth and pale, as though he spent too much time indoors. "She likes me to check over the rooms at the start of the season. Windows, screens, closet doors." He shrugged. "I do the carpentry."

"You're a carpenter?" she asked.

"Not by trade, no." He smiled, shaking his head slightly. He was tall and attractive, in a male-model kind of way.

"Well, look around," she said as she turned back to her suitcase and began to empty it onto the bed. First, she took out a black marble statue of a horse: the only meaningful remnant from her past, a birthday gift from Barbara, her foster mother. Then, with a shiver, she reminded herself—not quite the only remnant. There was something else, something that she'd have to face and deal with, something that wouldn't go away by her simply putting it out of her mind. She snorted—as if anything from her past ever really would.

She sorted her belongings. Two pairs of jeans. Two sweaters. Three shirts. Six panties. Three T-shirts. Two books. A zippered case of soap, shampoo, a comb, and toothpaste and brush. Everything new. Then her hands fell back onto the statue and she pushed it down into the soft bedcovers, as if willing it to disappear. Although she loved it, the associations it held for her were still too fresh, too raw.

The landlady's son cleared his throat and reported, "There's a hole in the window screen and some loose baseboard, and quarter round too." He pointed up toward the ceiling, which was made of that rough white stuff with silver sprinkles. "When would it be convenient for me to come in and fix—"

"You are in," she interrupted, suddenly resentful of an intrusion to which she'd given her permission. "Why didn't you come and do all this before I moved in?"

"Sorry, but I just finished my exams." He shrugged. "If you'd prefer that I didn't..."

"No." She shook her head. "I'll be out this afternoon." She realized it didn't matter. Even if he looked at her things, there was nothing he could discern from them. She was starting over, as anonymous as a cloud. "You can do it then."

CHAPTER 2

Once unpacked, Shadow decided to go for a walk to explore the area. After walking for several minutes down a long, quiet street, she noted a corner store where she planned to stop and buy food on her way back to the boarding house. Next she walked past a fancy brick building with hedges and statues in front. Then a few stores, vacant lots, and a few houses. The downtown was to the far left, but she continued straight, along a buckling, weed-infested sidewalk, walking steadily until she reached the river.

Which was immense. She'd never seen one like it. It was as though they'd taken the entire river valley in Edmonton, and then some, and filled it to the brim with raging water. Competing with the roar of the river were the frantic cries of gulls. Soaring above the spray, they dove headlong into the steel-grey, white-sliced river, then flapped up from the raging water to perch on the

Racing Shadows

concrete breakwall and gulp their catch. She leaned onto the thick wall which had been pleasantly warmed by the sun's rays and breathed in the smell of the river. The wall was broken down in many places, but not where she stood. Where she stood, it was strong.

There is a smaller river, just a creek really. Her foster mother is sitting by her side. Shadow has found a small fish, stuck in a puddle, cut off from the rest of the water; who knows how. Shadow uses one hand to dredge out the muck so the fish can escape. It darts away instantly as though it has been waiting. Barbara says, "The angel on your right shoulder saw that."

Shadow turns to look into her foster mother's eyes, which are a very deep brown, like her own, and returns her kind smile.

The rush of the river was intoxicating. So much power. There were waterfalls, Niagara Falls, miles downstream, to her left. Honeymoons, that's what came to her mind—brides in beautiful white gowns of the type that she herself would never own or wear. She sighed, and then turned her attention to the people fishing along the breakwall. She watched them casting in their lines and reeling them back, pulling out their catch with hand nets and throwing the fish into big water-filled buckets sitting alongside the wall.

She had trouble conceiving that the fish could survive in such a roiling, churning river. Maybe they were afraid, she imagined, maybe they grabbed the fishermen's hooks to get away from the raging water, not knowing their ultimate fate.

Oddly saddened, she heaved a deep sigh, turned around, and began walking back.

CHAPTER 3

Grey was Shadow's favorite color for horses. The filly she was leading was a beautiful dappled grey. Peter had called her: "the prettiest horse in the barn." Shadow agreed, but wished, instead, that she was the best behaved horse in the barn.

Shadow had once seen a drawing of the inside of a horse's body and the brain looked incredibly tiny compared with the rest of the animal—an ounce of brain to a thousand pounds of muscle and guts. Kiss n' Tell was proving herself true to that image. She was giving Shadow a very hard time. Twice the horse had slammed her in the face with her head, which was as long as Shadow's upper body and as solid as rock. The filly would not calm down; sweat dripped off her body like rain drops and frothed on her neck where Shadow leaned, trying to hold her back from running anyone down. Shadow patted her, and whispered in her ear, "Silly horse. Silly, silly horse. There's nothing wrong. Nothing is wrong and if you keep this up, someone is going to get hurt." Shadow's heart pounded in her throat wondering if they were going to make it to the race alive.

Finally, the filly settled, still bouncing and kicking a bit, but in control. Shadow glanced at her as they walked. She was proud to be leading her—a creature more beautiful than any human being could ever dream of being. And she felt one thing for certain. Kiss n' Tell was going to win her race.

Kiss's jockey was a woman. When thrown onto Kiss's back, she landed as lightly as a bird. Yet instantly, the filly crouched and leapt, as if trying to climb out from under her rider's touch. Shadow passed the lead shank to the pony-boy—*your problem now buddy*, she whispered under her breath. Then she turned, and headed for the grandstand, putting six dollars on the filly's nose at twelve to one. She loved the crowds of people in the grandstand. They were not like the crowds in stores or on city sidewalks. They were like her. They were untamed.

Shadow threaded her way through milling bodies, pungent cigars, and spilled beer, her new cowboy boots sticking to the tacky concrete floor with every step. She left the building, passed through a gate, and walked down to the dirt track, which was "good" today, almost "fast." She joined the others who had brought over horses, four men and a woman, there to watch the race and collect the horses afterward.

Shadow scanned them briefly, then looked away. She didn't want to talk to anyone: she wanted to concentrate on the race, on Kiss n' Tell. She wanted her to win. *You can do it, Kiss. Run, run for your life, just*

Racing Shadows

throw your legs out onto the air and run, she told the horse silently. *Win!*

The horses, topped by tiny riders in glistening silks, rode away from the stands; then they were behind the gate and Shadow couldn't see them any longer. She waited, as tense as the filly had been earlier, until the announcer's voice boomed, "They're at post. They're off!"

Shadow sucked in a deep breath and held it.

"And it's Kiss n' Tell breaking into the lead and moving across horses to the inside, Dandy Hero is running second, My Bluebird third, Rash Request is moving up between horses, Canadian Conquest fifth on the outside, and Fish for Dinner is trailing."

Please, Kiss. Please.

"And at the quarter pole, it's Kiss n' Tell by four, Dandy Hero second, My Bluebird losing ground, Rash Request and Canadian Conquest battling for fourth and, trailing, is Fish for Dinner."

Still holding her breath, Shadow squeezed her eyes shut: *Come on, Kiss, run. Don't stop now, you've got them!*

"In the stretch and down to the wire, Kiss n' Tell is running away with it; she's all alone! Behind her come Dandy Hero for second, Rash Request in third, and My Bluebird takes fourth position. Kiss n' Tell ran huge, taking the win by six!"

Kiss! Shadow pushed the stale air out of her lungs in a rush, gulping in the fresh so suddenly that she felt faint. People in the crowd yelped with joy or cursed, depending on how they'd bet. Kiss had won! To Shadow it seemed she'd almost been one with Kiss, as though some part of herself had been out on the track racing among the horses. And winning!

The riders were standing up in their stirrups now, high above the horses' backs, reining in their mounts. Shadow watched them bounce around the clubhouse turn, then took out her betting slip and looked at it, calculating her winnings. Seventy-odd dollars—not bad for a six-dollar bet.

When Kiss came back for her photo, legs flying, her head up as high as the grey clouds, her nostrils were flared wide and pouring blood.

"I'm really sorry," Shadow told Peter.

He was standing in the shed row. He'd changed into a suit and he looked sad. It made her feel for him, his grief.

"She was going to be a good horse. She was silly, but she was kind. She'd of been good," he said with a sigh.

"Yeah," Shadow agreed.

"Even if she never won a race, I'd have liked her. She had heart."

"I know."

"Owner gave me a hundred."

"Gave me fifty. And … I bet on her."

He turned to her and nodded once. "Good choice."

Racing Shadows

"My foster mother used to say that everything happened for a reason and that it was what God wanted," Shadow said.

Peter turned to her, looking surprised. "God wanted Kiss to die?"

"That's what she would have said: God's will."

He shook his head. "I could, just as an example, kill a man or not kill him, as my choice, and what would that mean? I could do either. Which would be God's will?"

"Whichever one you chose I guess."

"That makes no sense," he said, shaking his head.

"I didn't say I believe her," Shadow replied and sighed, not mentioning that she *had* believed her, for years.

Then he grinned at her, looking unbearably cute. "Do you think God wanted me to be this small?"

"Don't you like it?" she asked.

He laughed, his cheeks dimpling. His green eyes sparkled beneath dark eyebrows. His arms folded across the front of his dark jacket, he shrugged. "It doesn't leave me too many options in life."

"You could have joined the circus," she suggested, half joking, then added, "I always wanted to be in the circus."

"Why?" he asked, tilting his head as though he was actually interested in her answer.

"It's fun. People like it."

He shrugged. "People like horse racing."

"Yes," she agreed, feeling oddly guilty. *Of what?*

Later, after the day's work was all done, Shadow found herself squatting in the shed row, her back leaning against the cool concrete blocks, outside Kiss's empty stall. Peter joined her, but remained silent, chewing on a stalk of hay. She knew she could and should go home now. But she wanted to stay. She listened to him breathing in and out. He didn't seem to want to leave either. She wondered where he was going tonight, in his suit, but wouldn't ask him. She told herself to go home. Yet she stayed.

CHAPTER 4

Paul was in the front yard with the dog when Shadow finally got home from the track.

"Hi," he said. "Good day at the races?"

She shook her head. "Our horse died."

"Broke a leg?"

"Burst an abscess on her lung."

"That's tough."

"Yeah," she said as she crouched down and patted the dog's head. "What is he, an Australian Shepherd?"

"Maybe part. But just a Heinz 57, really."

"Well, he's very handsome, aren't you boy," she said as she got to her feet.

"Go on inside and get something to eat," Paul said. "Mom makes up a big pot of soup or stew every night. Help yourself. There's salad and home-make bread too. All you can eat."

"Oh, I didn't know that," she said. "How much does it cost?"

"It's more or less included in the rent," he replied.

"She didn't mention…."

"She tries to help out the women on the track: knows they're dirt poor and way outnumbered by the men, who get to live free in the tack rooms on the backside." He shrugged. "For years, she cooked for six children and a husband. I guess the habit's hard to break."

"It must be tiring for her," Shadow said.

"Nope. She's happiest in the spring and summer when the track is here. She gets lonely in the winter, forgetful. She forgets to eat, forgets to go to bed...." He shook his head. "Makes me worry."

They walked inside and to the kitchen where Mrs. Shevchuk sat in the corner, reading a book. The room was large, and full of shadows. As Paul ladled out vegetable soup and cut bread, Shadow fetched some salad and butter from the fridge. She tried to make some sense of the language that Paul and his mother were speaking, but couldn't: still, the sounds of the strange words pleased her.

Then, the rich food smells overcame her and she wolfed the salty, rich soup and the warm, crusty bread without paying attention to Paul and his mother until she noticed a change in the old woman's voice. She was trying to shout, her frail voice cracking.

Paul spoke to her quietly, but firmly. Still, she became more and more excited until she started to bang her fists on the arms of her chair. Paul was quickly at her side. He held her hands between his, and she stopped, her wide-open eyes shutting as she began to cry. The book fell from her lap as Paul helped her to her feet, then guided her up the stairs. Shadow watched

Racing Shadows

until she lost sight of the hem of the old woman's dark dress.

By the time Paul returned to the kitchen, Shadow had finished eating and had washed and dried her dishes. "Is she all right?"

He gave a short laugh. "Yeah. She gets confused sometimes. That's all."

Shadow began to ask what had suddenly confused the woman when she heard the front door opening. "Someone's coming," she blurted with a note of urgency.

"Don't worry. It's not the boogeyman," he chuckled, and she felt her cheeks burn.

A pretty blonde woman walked into the kitchen and stopped, hands on her hips, in front of Paul who was seated by the table. "When'd you get in?" she demanded. Without waiting for an answer, she straddled him, spread-eagled, her arms draping around his neck, and kissed him.

"This is Abby," Paul told Shadow once the woman had finished with him and was getting her food. His face registered surprise—as if he wasn't sure what was going on. He cleared his throat. "Abby's been living here for, what, five years?"

"I was the first boarder," she said, presumably to Shadow. "Got the best room. Upstairs, with a skylight and a fireplace, not that I use the fireplace an awful lot, but it gives it atmosphere, you know. You look like a good kid. I'll leave it to you when I die. Who did you say you work for?"

Surprised at the odd promise to bequeath her the room, Shadow stammered, "Ah … Billie Moon."

"Dude's got some good horses. You groomin' or ridin' or what?"

"I'm just walking hots right now."

"Jesus, that was lousy today, Billie's horse, that grey," Abby said, shaking her head. "I wasn't over there, but I heard about it; talk about rotten luck. She won it too."

Shadow watched her from the back as she cut the bread. Her waist was tiny. It looked as though Shadow could fit one hand around it.

Abby continued. "Filly collapsed before she got into the winner's circle. Gave Jessie, her jock, a real turn. I don't think Jessie will be back here tonight. I think she's staying with her boyfriend at the motel. He flew in to see her this week, maybe she won't even ride tomorrow. She's real touchy that way. She'd ride with a half-broken leg, but not right after she's been on a horse that got hurt. Bet it'll be a couple days before she can shake off that horror show."

Shadow nodded and waited for her to go on, but then she began eating and was silent for the first time since kissing Paul.

"This is Shadow, by the way," Paul said, taking advantage of her silence while it lasted.

Abby nodded. She was eating like it was a race.

"Are you a jockey too, Abby?" Shadow asked.

Racing Shadows

She didn't stop chewing to answer. "Nope. I hate coming out of the gate. Got caught up bad once. I won't even work one out of the gate anymore."

"That's understandable," Shadow said. She'd never been in the gate herself, in fact, had never ridden a horse at all, let alone a racehorse.

Abby wiped her mouth, having finished her meal in what seemed like seconds, and began talking to Paul again in what looked like a conspiratorial whisper.

She stopped talking when the outside door slammed. Boot heels clacked down the hall, and another woman entered the kitchen. She was almost the opposite of Abby, big and dark, with long, thick hair that was more the texture of a horse's mane than of human hair. She was introduced as Georgia, a groom. After nodding a hello, she got herself some soup and bread, then sat down and ate. Without saying a word.

"So how's the big vet doing? Got your working papers yet?" Abby asked Paul.

"Another year—if I pass my exams."

"Waddya doin' for the summer?"

"Working in town, at the clinic," he answered.

"Dogs and cats, right?"

"Yep."

"Well, I can't say as that's the most manly thing I've ever heard of," Abby replied, tut-tutting.

"Someone's got to do it," he offered.

"I suppose," Abby said. "Although five years ago, I had bigger things in mind for you."

"Dogs and cats are quite big enough for me. And they don't kick your brains out when you're trying to help them."

"Sorry," Abby said quickly. "I don't know where my head's at sometimes."

He turned to Shadow. "My dad trained horses. That was how he died, one well-placed kick."

For the first time, Georgia spoke. "Dead is dead and it don't do no good to worry it."

"He's probably better off than us," Abby added, "wherever he is."

Paul shrugged. "Could be."

"My … foster father was a vet," Shadow said. No matter how often she said the word, Shadow hated calling Tony her father, even with the word foster in front of it.

"Hey, that's a coincidence. Where?"

"He has a practice out west but he's trying to sell it. He had a job offer working for a drug company."

"That's where the money is."

"Yeah, and you don't have to worry about dissatisfied owners."

"And incompetent staff," Paul added.

"Or collecting overdue bills," Shadow retorted.

"Midnight calls," Paul added, shaking his head.

"So why are you doing this again, honey?" Abby asked, "If it's hard and doesn't pay a lot.

"I dunno. I'm just a fool I guess." He shook his head.

Racing Shadows

Abby rose to her feet, scraping back her chair. "If you get lonely or cold tonight, honey, just remember where I am, okay?" She winked and headed up the stairs, her jeaned bottom wagging. Mating call ... or just the way she walked?

Before Shadow could decide what to think, Georgia stood up, collected her own and Abby's dishes, and as she passed Paul on her way to the sink hissed, "Just try it."

Paul laughed out loud, leaving Shadow more puzzled than ever. "Good night," she said to him and to Georgia's back at the kitchen sink.

Georgia grunted.

"See you tomorrow," Paul said cheerily as if this had been the best evening he'd spent in a year. "Need a wake-up call?"

"Ah, no," Shadow responded.

"Good. Because I don't get up until eight. Eat your heart out!"

In her room, Shadow turned away from the mirrors as she stripped off her clothes and laid them neatly across the foot of the bed. Sliding between the covers and into the softness of the bed, she felt a deep and immediate comfort. She didn't understand why anyone would want to sleep on a hard mattress, no matter how healthy it might be. She felt that a bed should be like a nest, like a womb, the one place where you could forget about the world and your troubles.

She rolled toward the wall and closed her eyes. But the touch of sheets, the feel of them against her naked skin…

The amber girl screams, "Stop it! Help me." But nobody comes. Nobody helps her. The man starts to choke her. Once she stops struggling, he grabs both her hands in his and pins them above her head. Then he shoves her onto the floor. Shadow can almost feel the rough carpet against her back. Shadow doesn't want to watch, but her eyes refuse to look away. They keep watching for what will come next.

Shadow tried to hold back her tears, but they leaked out anyway. She got out of the bed, pulled on her jeans and shirt, then lay down on the bed again, but this time on top of the covers.

She tried to sleep, instead rolling and tossing—the bed now seeming more like a prison than a nest. Her throat felt parched and she wanted a drink. She got up to walk to the bathroom for one, and when she passed the living room, she saw Mrs. Shevchuk sitting in a chair. She appeared to be asleep, her grey head fallen onto one shoulder.

Quietly, Shadow tiptoed back to her room, took a blanket from her bed, and lowered herself into the chair next to the old woman's, pulling the plaid blanket over herself up to her chin. The sound of another person

Racing Shadows

breathing, steady, low, was comforting. The last thing Shadow saw before her eyes closed was the grey of the woman's hair.

She dreamt a river.

The amber girl breaks away from the man, running and running until she reaches the banks of a river. Realizing that she has finally escaped him, happiness washes over her. Shadow can feel the girl's relief.

The girl wades into the river, frolicking in the waves and sand.

Suddenly, the man reappears out of nowhere, beckoning her to join him on the shore.

Instead, the girl runs the other way, deeper and deeper into the water. The current begins to pull her down. Shadow screams for the girl to come back to shore, but she doesn't. Shadow is too afraid to jump in and save her. The amber girl disappears beneath the water's surface.

Shadow awoke to see Mrs. Shevchuk bending over her, stroking Shadow's hair back from her forehead, as if Shadow were a small child who had a fever. She began to speak, but Shadow didn't understand the foreign words.

"I'm all right," Shadow explained. "I had a bad dream."

"Yes. Only bad dream," she said, her lips pulling back in a smile.

Shadow tried to smile back but it was hard.

"Nobody will hurt you here," Mrs. Shevchuk said as she pulled at Shadow's arm, then guided her back to her room. She folded back the bed covers and once Shadow was in the bed, lifted and smoothed them gently over her.

"Pleasant dreams," she said. Crossing the room, she grasped a chair and dragged it over to Shadow's bed. "I stay right here and won't let nothing and nobody bother you."

CHAPTER 5

When Shadow awoke early the next morning, she watched as Mrs. Shevchuk left her room with a nod and a smile. Shadow mouthed, "Thank you," as the woman closed her door. Then Shadow sat up in bed and looked out her window, searching the yard for Squeaks' coat, but couldn't see it. He was probably inside his dog house. She gazed past the lawn and across the street to the track's backside to see lights glinting in a few barns. Deciding there was no point in delaying, she pulled on her clothes and stole out the door, closing it softly behind her.

As she crunched down the gravel driveway, past Squeaks' dog house, she heard him woof low in his sleep. It was just past five, still dark, and so quiet that miles away, she could hear the river breathe. The air lay dark and damp around her, muffling the quick solid *thunk* of her boot heels on the asphalt road, as they propelled her on, down the dark street. In front of her, obscuring the gate and veiling the guard's hut in a golden haze, rested a light fog.

The guard asked to see the pass for which she'd been photographed and fingerprinted yesterday morning. As she flashed it, she noted the traces of black ink remaining on the tips of two of her fingers and a thumb. In one corner of the laminated pass, below her unsmiling face, sat her thumbprint. It looked criminal, as if she'd finally been caught.

The track backside was not as quiet as it had seemed from a distance. Ahead, she heard voices raised in dispute, muffled as though behind a closed door. Then, suddenly, from behind her came the flurry of shod hooves spitting gravel and the sharp cry, "Loose horse! Loose horse!"

She turned, too late—he'd already passed her. But when she whistled, he hesitated, and turned his head, a long leather shank streaming back across his dark flank like the tail of a kite as he ran. Suddenly, people appeared spread across the road in front of him, waving arms and whistling. He jerked to a stop and was caught.

Shadow continued on to the kitchen. There was plenty of room to sit this morning. She sat at an empty table by the windowed wall, and set down her tray of oatmeal, juice, and a boiled egg. As she ate, she watched the other people from a distance. They were all men, young and old. She amused herself by guessing, from their appearance, their jobs.

The smallest, bent over a racing form, was a jockey. The tall, thin one galloped. The muscular one with the beard might be a groom, but he was wearing a helmet, so he must be a pony boy. The old ragged ones, grey and raw-boned and stirring their coffees were grooms. The gangling kid walked hots. The ones wearing dress

Racing Shadows

pants and sporty jackets were the trainers. They were the worried ones, with wrinkles in their eyes, who couldn't afford to stir and stare. They gulped and ran. She glanced out the window. The one getting out of the Cadillac was a vet.

She and they were all here for the same reason: for the horses.

Back at her barn, a light fell from one stall, illuminating the shed row in front of it. Shadow walked up and leaned into the doorway to find Peter brushing off a horse. "Got a walker for you," he said without turning, as though he knew she'd be early.

"Great," she said and the bay, who was looking the other way, turned to stare at her with his handsome white face.

Peter slipped the chain of the lead shank through the colt's mouth and snapped it. "I think he'll be good for you, but he hates the east corner," Peter told her. "And he bites."

"I remember you from yesterday, Charley," she said, rubbing her right arm on which he'd left at least three sets of bruises. She snapped open the webbing and took the shank from Peter.

"Just try it today," she warned the horse as she led him along the shed row. "I'm wise to you now." The brute rolled his eye. He saw her watching him and understood.

The horses were all more difficult on the days that they hadn't been worked under saddle, on the days they only walked. At the east corner, he reared and she stepped aside, his bulk churning above her. He was a tall horse, his withers clearing the top of her head, probably the tallest horse she'd yet handled.

The leather of the shank felt smooth and right beneath her hand. Charley walked quickly, but he responded to the chain through his mouth, his neck arching to the pressure, and didn't try to drag her like some horses did, a relief because her muscles were sore from yesterday: it'd been months since she'd walked a horse. She couldn't take her eyes off him though, or he'd strike out fast as a snake and bite her, then jerk away before she could counter. She found that keeping up her guard was easier today.

Over and over she passed Peter, who was mucking out the stall. Methodically, he piled manure and soiled straw onto an outspread feed sack. When it was full, he pulled the corners of the rough brown cloth together, compressing the contents. Then he hefted the bulging mass onto his shoulder and carried it across the ditch and to the manure pile, where he dumped it. Each time Shadow passed him, she wondered what he was thinking about, she wondered if he was bored, and if he ever wanted to do this with his life, or if he simply had no other choice.

For although he was small, it was clear that he couldn't ride races. He was a dwarf, not a perfect miniature man, like the jockeys were, but differently proportioned, his arms and legs shortened, his torso and head large in comparison.

Racing Shadows

He was more than his short physique, though. Peter would have loved Kiss even if she'd never won a race because she had heart and heart was something very separate from structure or speed. Shadow didn't know exactly what it was, but she'd felt it too—the marvel. She'd felt it in Kiss and now, in Peter too.

People had started to arrive at the barn; there was laughter and bustle, and rain began pouring from the still-dark and starless sky. By the time she had put one of Peter's horses back into its stall, another had come off of the track. She'd hold it while Peter washed off the mud and sweat with buckets of warm water that smelled of pine disinfectant, which was what the horses smelled of—pine—not like animals at all.

Wet to the skin, Shadow grew cold and cramped. She could feel a headache creeping up her spine and closing in on the back of her skull. Because there was no racing that afternoon, she knew that when she was done the morning's work, she could go home, grab a hot shower, and crawl into her bed. She held that thought ahead of her like a beacon to keep her swimming—she'd never felt so tired. When Peter's horses were all finished, she entered a stall into which she'd just seen a horse and rider walk. When she arrived, the rider was down and had pulled off his saddle. The groom handed him the bridle, and Shadow stepped aside to let the rider pass, his white teeth flashing an astonishing smile from out of his mud-pie face.

"I'll take him for you," Shadow said to the groom, who had haltered the horse. Looking her up and down, he grunted. He was tall and muscular in a spare sort of way, and his slick, blue-black hair fell to his shoulders. All he wore above his tight jeans was a grey undershirt, badly torn.

She led the mud-caked horse out of the shed to the steaming water buckets the groom had prepared, noting that beneath the mud, the horse was black. "What's his name?" she asked when the groom arrived.

He plucked a sponge from the steaming bucket. "Leprosy," he said against the horse's neck. Shadow could smell the whiskey from where she stood at the horse's head.

"Leprosy?" she asked.

"Yeah. He's only got three legs."

She looked down at the horse's legs and, in fact, one tendon was bowed. "Oh," she replied.

"Piece o' shit," the groom said then, kicking up into the horse's soft belly. The horse grunted and jumped aside.

"That won't make him any sounder!" Shadow hissed, moving between the man and the horse, who was now trying to get away from her, pulling at the shank, while the groom glared at her, began to speak, but changed his mind. Instead, he lifted the bucket and tossed the remaining water over the horse ... and her. Between wiping at the disinfectant burning her eyes and trying to calm down the horse, she heard him chuckle.

"Sorry," he said, still laughing. Apparently, she'd made his day. Almost cheerfully now, he took a scraper to the water and mud remaining on the horse.

Racing Shadows

"Finished," he said. Shadow turned and led the animal back into the shed row.

"Crowe!" a sharp voice called. "Where's that horse's cooler?" She turned to see Billie Moon striding toward her. He was wearing a red baseball jacket and checked slacks. His grey-streaked black hair was combed to one side, covering his missing eye, his face like a battle-scarred cat's. She wondered briefly why, once they'd seen Billie in the flesh, anyone would trust him with their valuable horses. The only explanation she could think of was his shining record, and maybe the old story that Indians have some mystical way with horses.

"I'm getting it," Crowe retorted. "I'll have it on him as soon as the bitch makes a turn."

"Just see to it, boy," Billie said as he walked over to the groom. Then, "This shed is a shit pile." He kicked at some dirty straw. "There's oats in the ditch!"

She was too far away then to make out the rest. When she came back around, Billie was holding out a cooler and spread it onto the horse's back, looping it over his ears and tying it at the base of his neck. He ran a hand across the horse's chest and brought it up muddy. "Lazy son-of-a-bitch," he muttered.

"How's he walking?" he asked Shadow.

"Stiff, but he's not limping."

"Don't stop him too long," he warned her.

"Yes, sir."

Billie turned back to the groom. "You're bloody useless, you know that? You don't even bounce anymore. What time you start today? You're going to be the last one finished. You make sure you do up every horse today or it's your last day, you hear me? Damn!"

Then Shadow was out of earshot. When she came around again, she asked where the horse's water was. Crowe gave her a black look she felt right down into her gut.

"Get the damn water out!" Billie shouted when he overheard her question. She began to lead the horse past him, but he put a hand on her shoulder. "Little girl," he said, "I've got two more jobs for you." He raised the brow above his good eye and held her there uncomfortably.

"Yes, sir," she said, squirming slightly.

"I want you to look after the pony and I want you to get this bastard out of the sack the minute you get here each morning!"

With that, he released his grip on her shoulder and she walked on. When she came back around, the water bucket was hung up on the rail and Billie was gone. Leprosy, or whatever his real name was, slurped up five big gulps before she could pull him away.

Eventually, Crowe yanked off the horse's cooler and disappeared into a stall. She continued walking until it seemed as though she'd been walking the horse for a lifetime. Her head was pounding so hard that she couldn't focus her eyes. She saw everything in a haze, in twos and threes. Stopping at each stall, she looked for Crowe. Finally, she found him wrapping up a horse's legs in thick cotton bandages. "Can I put him away

Racing Shadows

now?" she asked. "He's dry and cool and he's stopped drinking."

Without looking up, the man shook his head.

She sighed and kept walking. On her next turn, Peter stepped out of a stall in front of her. He put up his hand, signaling her to stop the horse, then stepped closer and rubbed his hand across the animal's chest and between the twin muscles above its legs. "Put him to bed," he told her.

After she'd refilled the water bucket and hung it in Leprosy's stall, she wandered back to Peter's stalls. She found him inside one, putting on bandages, and she leaned against the open doorway, running her hands along the nylon webbing spanning it, and watched him work. He turned his head when he was finished the leg he was working on. "All done?" he asked her.

"I'm supposed to look after the pony," she told him. "Where is he? I've seen him, but I can't find him now."

"He's in another barn. If you wait a while, I'll take you to him. Come on in."

She ducked under the webbing and sat in a corner. The straw was soft and she began to feel better. The cramping in her shoulders eased and some warmth began to seep back into her stiff bones. She watched the horse pull hay from a net as Peter worked.

"Who's this?" she asked.

"Copper Light. We got her in a week ago. Guy claimed her in a race where she ran dead last. He got her cheap and was sure her problem was her trainer. Figures Billie'll have her winning in a month."

"What do you think?" Shadow asked, looking her over. She was a small chestnut, coppery bright as a new penny, and very pretty with her small shapely ears and broad forehead tapering to a refined muzzle. A thin blaze ran all the way down her face. Topping off all that were streaks of lustrous silver running through her mane and tail.

"Well, that's how Billie made his reputation. He started off with cripples and horses nobody else would waste their time on, built 'em up, and won with 'em."

"Oh," she said. "Is she sore?"

"Nope, not this one. She just doesn't know how to run yet."

"Hmmm," she said. The sharp smell of liniment stung her nostrils as she listened to the faint chafe of Peter's hands scuffing across the filly's leg. She closed her eyes for a few minutes and when she opened them again, her headache was gone.

"How many horses do you groom?" she asked as he kept working.

"I rub five. Billie gave me Crowe's stakes filly yesterday to make up for Kiss. Crowe ain't happy about it. She was his only good one. Then I have Charley."

"He's a pretty good horse, isn't he?" she broke in.

He nodded. "Runs for a twenty thousand dollar tag. And I've got that black filly from Crowe now. She's by Northern Racer. Then the roan—he ran in the Prince of Peace Stakes last year. Then that other chestnut mare by Good Old Hero."

Racing Shadows

"I'm impressed," she said. He seemed to have all the best horses in the barn.

Peter rose to his feet, slapping the little filly's shoulder. She turned to nuzzle him and he laughed. "I'm not so sure about you," he said to the horse. "I think you'd make some little girl a nice pony. I think you've found yourself the wrong job."

"She does seem quiet."

"Too quiet," he agreed as they left the stall. "Now let's go find you that pony. Follow me."

Two barns over stood their large Appaloosa pony, tied to a rail, and still wearing his saddle.

"When you're done walking horses," Peter said, "you unsaddle, groom, and muck him out, then put him away with hay and water."

"A bath?"

"Only when he's dirty—like today. Otherwise, just brush him off and pick out his feet. If he's needed in the afternoon, the pony-boy will saddle him again. Do you ride, by the way?"

She shook her head. "Nope."

"Too bad," he said. "Or I'd let you ride my walkers bareback. It's easier than walking 'em."

She gave him a sharp look. "Why would you?"

"Why would I what?"

"Do me a favor?"

He shrugged. "I don't envy you your job."

She narrowed her eyes at him.

53

"Whenever someone new starts," he explained, "Billie gives them the job of getting Crowe up. It's kind of like a test to see how much they want to work here."

She sighed. Her feet were pounding hot inside her new boots and she could feel a spot on each heel rubbed raw and stinging. "Remind me to learn to ride last year," she said.

He smiled. "And because I can tell you love them."

"Love them?"

"The horses."

She tilted her head and examined him, suspicious of anyone who tried to tell her how she felt. Then, despite herself, she surrendered a smile.

He grinned back. "In the morning, saddle the pony first thing when you get in."

"You mean after I get Crowe out of bed," she said, thinking back to the way Crowe looked at her when Billie gave the order, his knowing leer.

"Yes, after." Peter tipped his head back to look up at her. "Be careful," he warned, then added, "and yell for me if you have a problem. I'm two doors over." As she tried to decide whether his statement made her feel in any way safer, he turned and headed back across the new, mud-stained grass.

"Bye," she called after him, wishing he'd stay. He raised a hand in response without turning.

Suddenly, anger flashed through her. Who was he to be so rude? First, he pretended to like her, made her begin to feel accepted here, and now he was suddenly cold, walking away from her without a word.

Racing Shadows

Feeling her eyes burning with rising tears, she turned to the pony and pressed her face into his thick, speckled neck. In turn, the animal breathed in deeply and sighed, as though comforting young women was just his lot in life, a burden that, as a gentleman, he must simply bear. Again, he sighed.

"Oh, all right," she said, sniffing. She wiped away her tears and pulled off his saddle, leaving him tied him to the post outside. "Wait here," she said.

It had stopped raining hard, but a few drops were still falling, prickling in the brown puddles that seemed to lie everywhere. She didn't like leaving the pony outside, but she'd rather not have him in the stall while she worked—she didn't want to slip and stab him with the fork. Nervously, she wondered if he'd be all right outside … then she looked down at herself and laughed. Her shirt was so wet it was stuck to the skin of her breasts and stomach, her hair plastered in strands across her cheeks and throat. And she was worried about the horse? Of course he'd be okay.

Smiling, she fetched a manure basket and filled it as quickly as possible. All the horse's droppings were piled in one corner of the stall and all the urine-soaked straw was in the centre of it, so much of the straw was still clean. When she'd dumped the last of the soiled straw onto the manure pile, she realized she'd have to go back to the barn for another bale of straw. As she began to head over, she saw Peter hauling a bale her way. Stood on its end, it was as tall as him.

IA Moore

When he arrived, he broke the bale and carried half of it into the stall. She was so happy he hadn't abandoned her that she suddenly wanted to run or dance.

Instead, she speared a thick flake on her pitchfork and twisted it quickly, to and fro, spilling out the golden-yellow straws into the horse-scented air. Peter stood near her as the straw settled to the ground, high and soft, like a blanket or like … Rumplestiltskin, of course; the maiden spinning the straw into gold and the crazy little man. She began to laugh. He joined her.

When she stopped laughing, her eyes were moist and she regarded him through the haze. His lips curved up against his black moustache and the dimples of his cheeks, his baggy pants falling in soft folds from his hips to the tops of his hiking shoes. Beneath his cap, above his beard, his ears were perfect shells. She wanted to touch them….

"Billie tells me you're half Indian," he said.

She shrugged, staring at him. "Make love to me," she said.

"Here? Now?" His eyes darkened, softened: they seemed larger.

Still holding the fork in one hand she folded her arms across her chest, squeezing herself as tight as she could. Not breathing. "Yes," she whispered.

"Why?" he asked, his brows drawn together.

She couldn't speak. She felt her lips break apart as if to try. Seconds passed.

Racing Shadows

"No," he said, but stepped toward her, holding out his open hand for hers.

She clenched the four-pronged, needle-tined fork in her right hand, felt its weight.

Tony loves to torment Shadow. He sends Barbara out of the house, to the store to fetch something they do not have at home. At first, she fools him by stocking everything, but he's smart. He asks for things she'd never think of: a hoe (they have no garden), ice-skate laces (they don't skate), filter paper for a coffee maker (the kind they don't have). His requests become more and more ridiculous, but she always obeys him. She never asks Shadow what happens when she's gone. Perhaps she actually doesn't want to know.

Without thinking about what she was doing, Shadow flipped the fork up sideways, catching the handle's neck in her left hand, holding the fork like a bar across her chest. Rage draped her in a burning cloak.

Taking a quick step forward, she lunged at Peter with the wooden handle. She wanted to push him away—push love, push hate, push all of it out of her life. He stepped aside, easily avoiding the fork, then ducked under the handle as she pulled in her arms, holding him trapped tightly against her body. She felt her muscles tremble. Peter shifted against her and she loosened her grip to let him move. His thick-veined hands slipped under her shirt, warm against her wet and clammy skin.

"No," he repeated in the same gentle voice.

Shadow's fists unclenched and the fork dropped into the straw.

Peter backed away, his hands falling away from her breasts like petals.

CHAPTER 6

Shadow woke from her nap to the sound of claws scuttling across wood and a bumping along the outside of her wall, followed by furious, high-pitched barking. Someone had just let Squeaks into the house, probably Paul. She turned over onto her stomach. Her headache was gone and her pillow was soft and fragrant where her freshly washed hair had been pressing. She felt pleasantly warm. Pushing the covers off, she stretched, then looked down at her body, which was flat as the prairie, the color of amber, and downed in fine dark hair.

"Please don't," the amber girl begs, trembling in fear. She looks up at the man towering over her, then above him toward the sky. "Please, no."

He places his hands around her neck and runs his big thumbs up and down her delicate throat. "Then stop teasing me," he says. Tears fill her eyes as he begins to squeeze, silencing her words. "It's your own fault, you whore."

Shuddering, Shadow climbed out of bed. Then she dressed in clean jeans and T-shirt and walked out the front door, where she sat down on a step, and brush-dried her hair in the early-evening sun. Up close, even she found it pretty—the strands a mixture of colors, from black to red to blonde—combined together making a dark brown with glints of gold.

A car drove up the narrow driveway, swung to the left and parked on the grass. It was painted a bright shiny red over smoothed-out dents. Abby climbed out of the front seat, which Shadow saw was leopard-print. Another girl exited a rear door and after her came a man.

"Hi, Shadow. This is Jessie and her boyfriend, Carlos," Abby said. Shadow remembered her then—she was the jockey who rode Kiss in her race. She looked so different today in her slinky black dress than she'd looked in racing silks. The man wore a dark suit and Shadow thought he looked like a gangster.

"Wha's happenin'?" slipped from the side of his wide and slightly smiling mouth as he slung his arm over Jessie's shoulder.

"Hi," Shadow said, thinking how much she'd hate some man doing that to her.

"We were at the falls," Abby babbled on happily. "They're incredible! I never get tired of them, we went clean underneath—all that spray, it's so super, then we went to the wax museum and up in the tower and then shopping." She held up a statue of a moose in one hand

and a tiny birch canoe in the other. "See? You should come with us one time, Shadow. We could go at night when the lights change colors over the falls, it would be a blast—"

They all disappeared into the house with Abby still enthusing about their little trip, leaving Shadow alone again.

Peter had shown her the location of Crowe's room before she left the track earlier and in her mind's eye, she could still see its narrow white door when she closed her eyes. Her heart raced and stomach clenched just thinking about tomorrow morning and waking up Crowe. She thought about not going, about quitting.

Billie had no idea how difficult it would be for her to wake up Crowe. He probably thought that just because she could walk confidently into a thousand-pound horse's stall, that she could face… She considered calling him and telling him, begging for a reprieve but decided it would be futile—how could he, or anyone else really, understand?

She sighed. She could always look around for another job. *No!* she told herself. *I won't run away this time … not anymore, not ever!* She breathed a sigh of relief having come to a decision.

The door opened behind her and Squeaks bolted down the steps, then turned like a boomerang, and flung himself onto her lap. "Here, Squeaks!" Paul's voice commanded. "Here!" She pushed the dog off and wiped at her cheek where he'd run his long tongue. Paul snapped a leash onto the dog's collar.

"We're going for a walk. Want to come?"

"Where?"

"Along the power line, back in the woods. I can let him run there—no cars."

She shrugged. "Sure."

"You can work up an appetite."

Her stomach felt like a very deep and empty pit. "I'm not sure I need to do that," she said, smiling.

They made their way down the path between their house and the one beside it, back past the yards and long gardens. The ground was still wet, but the sun was finally out and everything looked deliciously green and new. As soon as they reached the power line, Paul unfastened the dog's leash and he bolted.

"He's pretty fast."

"Very," she agreed. "Who walks him when you're gone?"

"Nobody. He's going to be stiff tomorrow. Yesterday, I left him on the lead. Hey, I'm sorry. I forgot that you walk all morning."

"Oh, that's okay; this is different. I don't have half a ton of horse pulling on my shoulder." She rubbed her right shoulder.

"Hey, stop," he said. As if just now seeing her arms, he grabbed one in both of his hands. "They could use you in a shrink's office to do those Rorschach tests." He poked at one her bruises with his finger. "That one looks like a naked lady, no, a dancer in the Klondike gold rush; her name's Kate and she came up north to

Racing Shadows

escape her wicked uncle, yes, I can see it all here and she meets this handsome young prospector named—"

"Give me my arm!"

He released it.

"Anyway, you're wrong." She looked down at her bruised skin, squinting. "It's only a cat. Without ears. They were frozen off one winter when his cruel owner Howard kicked him out of the house for peeing in the Christmas cactus. So there."

"Nope, that's the one over here!" He jabbed at another of her bruises.

"Ouch!"

He began to laugh.

"I'm glad you think my pain is so funny," she said.

"What do you girls see in racehorses anyway? I mean, I can understand the guys. They start on the track hoping, against all the odds, I might add, to make big bucks. Or they enjoy being macho enough to risk their lives a dozen or so times a day. "But what about you girls? What's in it for you?"

"None of your business."

"Come on. Explain yourself."

"Why should I tell you anything?"

"Ah hah! You don't know."

"I do so! It's because we love the horses. They're ... beautiful."

"So?"

"And strong and powerful and they represent ... freedom."

"They're hardly free."

"Freedom restrained."

"Look at Squeaks there; he's man's best friend. He'd never bite you."

"He's one hundred per cent tamed!" she retorted as if that were an unforgivable flaw.

"And you'd rather commune with something that's half-wild?"

She shrugged, then sighed. "I love their power! When I was a kid, I'd crawl around on my hands and knees half the day, rearing and snorting." She laughed at herself, remembering. "I'd pretend I was Silver."

"Silver?"

"Yeah, the Lone Ranger's horse, before the Lone Ranger caught and tamed him, when he was still wild and led a herd."

"So you work at the track in kind of a vicarious sense?"

"Oh, God. Why are you asking me these stupid questions?" She turned to give him an angry look and his grin told her he was just teasing. She tightened her hand into a fist and punched his upper arm. It was thick with muscle.

"Beautiful … And strong!" he said.

She jerked her head up, as though surprised, looking into the distance. "Look! Over there!" she yelled, pointing. When he turned, she bolted in the opposite direction, her boots digging into the soft ground, legs and arms pumping as hard as they could. Within a few seconds, she heard him running behind her. She pushed harder, but then started to laugh, which slowed her.

Racing Shadows

Paul's weight hit the back of her legs and she plunged, arms outstretched, to the ground, her face pushed into the damp, fragrant weeds, his bulk suddenly on top of her, beginning to turn her over …

At first, he doesn't hurt the amber girl too badly. At first, he says he cares about her and is preparing her for life, training her for the future. It isn't until he actually penetrates her that she realizes ... how wrong it really is. As time goes on it gets even worse and all she can do is try to avoid him. Which is futile. Initially, she is too young to leave, and later she simply loves her foster mother too much to go.

… and just when she was about to heave him off of her, Squeaks showed up, frantic, licking them both as they laughed.

"Off! Down!" Paul yelled, but Squeaks refused to stop his hysterics until they got to their feet.

She stood with her hands on her hips, staring at him. "You idiot!"

"You started it!" he retorted.

"Look at me!" she said. "I'm covered in dirt now!"

"Come here. I can fix that."

She relaxed, the tightness in her muscles seeming to melt as they took turns at brushing mud and dried weeds off each other's clothes. She liked him but had to be honest. She rubbed her palms together. "You're being very nice and I appreciate you as a friend."

"But that's all," he interrupted. "You just want to be friends. Right? No more. No less."

"Well, yes, but you make it sound … so trite and worthless."

"I don't mean to," he said. "Good friends are hard to find, and I think you and I could be that," he finished.

She blushed. "Um, thanks. I hope that too. And anyway I thought after last night that you and Abby were a thing … or …"

"Two years ago, I asked Abby to marry me."

Shadow was surprised: Someone wanted to marry Abby? That sounded as likely as someone wanting to take a python to bed. "And?"

"And she said … she said no."

"Oh."

"Believe it or not, last night was the first time she and I have spoken since we split. All last summer was like ice. Now, I don't know what to think or do."

Shadow cleared her throat. "I don't mean to be a party-pooper, but I got the impression that Georgia is pretty much against you messing with Abby."

"Georgia's paranoid. She thinks she has to save Abby from me." He laughed, without humor. "I guess she had her reasons … once," he admitted. He cleared his throat. "Abby didn't actually just say 'No' when I asked her to marry me—what she actually said was, 'Don't be such an asshole,' and knocked the ring I was holding out to her onto the floor. That hurt … so I slapped her." He shook his head and gave a wry laugh. "And Georgia laid me out cold. I deserved it. And I'll never forget it."

They'd begun walking again. Squeaks romped ahead of them, poking his head into every bush, digging and sending clods of mud and grass flying out between his hind legs.

"Well, to me, it seems like she's forgotten, or at least forgiven." Shadow looked at him walking beside her, his handsome profile.

He grunted in a preoccupied way and they walked on silently, Shadow wondering if he'd be as sorry for what he'd done if it hadn't been for Georgia.

Finally, he cleared his throat. "So what do you think?"

She shrugged her shoulders. "About what?"

"You think she'll ever marry me?"

"How long has she been on the track?"

"Fifteen … sixteen years."

"I didn't know she was that old."

"She's thirty-five."

She shrugged. "Trackers are different from other people. They're half gypsies. You know that. The only thing the bunch of them have in common is the horses—for many of them, horses grow to be their whole world, the only thing they know and care about. Period!"

He sighed and nodded.

"You're not like that. She is though. Maybe that's why she told you not to be such an asshole. She knew you knew, but you wouldn't admit it. She's a tracker. Face it—you'd be sick of her in a year. What does she know besides horses?"

His answer was gruff, and thick with emotion. "I love her. I think she's wonderful. She's brave, she's strong. I've never met another woman like her."

Shadow was about to laugh. She'd heard the word "love" too often to believe it easily. Then something made her stop. After a long pause, she said, "She's got heart?"

"That's what my dad used to say when a horse was special."

"And to you, Abby is special that same way?"

Paul nodded. "Yes, exactly!"

As they turned to go back to the house, Paul whistled for Squeaks who ran to them, eating up ground like a locomotive. He sprang up onto Paul, causing him to half-stagger backward.

"So, what do you think? Should I try again?" he asked when he'd recovered his balance.

She snorted. "If only you knew who you were asking."

"You left somebody to come here, didn't you?" Paul asked. "I know a lonely heart when I see one."

She shrugged, then nodded. She did—she left Barbara, the only mother she'd ever known. A sob escaped her lips.

"I'm sorry. If you ever want to talk to someone..."

"Yeah, sure," she said, and thought about asking him about her pregnancy, what she should do about it.

Racing Shadows

She felt that she and Paul had made a connection, and she wanted to tell someone about the baby. But she couldn't force the words out. Not yet.

When they arrived at the front steps, about to head into the house for dinner, Abby came out the door, carrying a heaping dish of meaty dog food. She must have been waiting for them to return.

"Mmmm," she said, "just smell that aroma. It doesn't smell so good on the hoof, does it Squeaky boy? You don't know what you're getting here, could be something special tonight, could be a very well-bred dinner."

Shadow walked into the house alone. Abby might have positive qualities, but good taste wasn't one of them. As if she had heard Shadow's thoughts, Abby called after her.

"If we take life serious all the time, we'll end up, each and every one of us, throwing ourselves over the falls, God, sometimes there seems enough reason to."

As Shadow pulled the door closed behind her, she shook her head: love truly was blind.

The next morning began with soft air blowing through the open window onto Shadow's skin, fear throbbing in her veins, and Crowe on her mind.

The special bounce in Abby's manner that morning told Shadow Abby didn't spend the night alone. She looked so ... loved. Shadow felt a sudden ache.

Over coffee, she, Georgia, and Abby spoke about horses, of course: medicines, schedules, and race results. Several times though, Abby glanced dreamily up the stairs which surprised Shadow as otherwise Abby seemed so tough, not one to be sentimental.

Shadow took a ride to work in Abby's red car, which she said was a Mustang, only because there was no car called a Thoroughbred. Shadow got out at the gate, her arms and legs shaking slightly as she walked to the barn, her mind focused on the distasteful task that lay ahead of her. When she arrived at the barn, the work day had started. She could see a horse, dim in the morning mist, drifting off toward the track, maybe Peter's roan. A pony stood ground-tied in the yard, picking grass.

Shadow stopped short and stared at the slender door of Crowe's room. She wondered if he was really asleep or if he was ready, standing behind the door, waiting for her.

She spotted Peter near his stalls, up at the head of the barn, too far away. He waved. She waved back. Then she lifted her hands to her face and blew on them, attempting to warm them. Although the rest of her body felt hot and there was sweat trickling from her armpits down her sides, her hands were lumps of ice. And she couldn't seem to stop shaking. She stepped gingerly onto the sidewalk that ran in front of the rooms as a calico cat nipped between her legs. Normally she'd have called her back and petted her, but today there was no time for that kind of thing. The first thing she was supposed to do was to get "the bastard" out of the sack. She hadn't forgotten.

Racing Shadows

Early in the morning, the man creeps into the amber girl's room. Why doesn't she scream? Why doesn't she fight?

Shadow stood at the door of Crowe's room. She was unsure if she should knock first or just open the door. And she didn't know what she should do if he remained in bed, refusing to get up. She knocked once. No response. Knocked twice. Same result.

She tried the doorknob; the room wasn't locked. After turning it all the way, she pushed the door open. Through the lightening dark, she could make out his shape on the bed, black hair spread on a white pillow. *Like serpents*, she thought. She switched on the bare bulb hanging from the ceiling, revealing the heaped magazines, dirty clothes, old fast-food containers, and bottles of beer that littered the room. She cleared her throat loudly. Still, he didn't move. "Time to get up!" she said in a voice as strong as she could muster.

Fast as a snake, Crowe reached under his bed and pulled out a gun, pointing it at her as he rose onto an elbow. She stood frozen, steeling herself for the blast. But nothing happened. Grunting, Crowe shoved the weapon back under his cot. Then, groping under his pillow, he pulled out a flat bottle.

Laying back on the pillow again, he guzzled the amber liquid inside like a baby drinking its bottle.

"Time to get up!" she said, fearing that he'd drink himself into a stupor and she'd have failed to prove herself to Billie Moon, to Peter, to herself. In response, Crowe leapt to his feet, naked, the now empty bottle clattering onto the wooden floor.

Automatically, she backed up, bumping the edge of the door, which was ajar.

"Stupid bitch!" Crowe's hand shot past her shoulder, slamming the door shut behind her as he grabbed her hair with his other hand. Holding her hair fast in one fist, he turned her, then twisted one of her arms behind her back. Digging his knee into her spine, he forced her to her knees. Then he pushed her farther downward until she lay flat on the filthy floor. Prostrate before him. Once again, she was helpless and alone—the pain of it raking through her like pitchfork tines.

Suddenly he was flat on top of her, his tongue playing at the nape of her neck as she tried to buck him off her back. He laughed and forced her face harder against the rough floor boards.

The door creaked open. Her cheek pressed flat against the gritty floor, she couldn't turn to see who was there. A glint of hope rushed through her—maybe someone would save her from this indignity. When she tried to pull her arm away from Crowe, her shoulder screamed in pain. Her free hand searched under the cot directly in front of her, finally touching metal.

Crowe's gun! She felt … surprise, and a new strength flowed through her. Maybe this was what she'd been heading toward, her destiny. But before she could

Racing Shadows

do anything with the gun, Crowe wrenched it out of her grasp. The last thing she remembered was the bullet hitting her back like a sledge hammer. Her last thought was of her unborn child.

CHAPTER 7

Shadow woke to someone stroking her forehead with something cool. When she opened her eyes, she saw white, all white—and streaming through a crack between heavy curtains, a silver column of light. *I'm in a hospital,* she realized. Then her eyes focused on a dark shape hovering above her.

"Peter?" she croaked before her eyelids fell closed again.

"Yes. It's me."

His voice sounds so real. Or is it just another dream?

"Is this real?" she asked, opening her eyes again and trying to focus.

"It's real," he assured her. "Now that you're awake, I'll go get a nurse."

"No!" she said quickly. "Stay. Please. I feel fine." She actually felt like there was nothing beneath her skin but shredded meat and bone. But she was desperate for him to stay with her.

"You've been unconscious for days, and the doctor wants to be notified as soon as you're awake. He needs to talk to you."

Racing Shadows

"No," she said, terrified to let him go. "Please don't get him yet. I'm scared. Just stay here a minute. Please."

He nodded, as though he understood her fear. "It's all right, you know," he said. "Everything's all right." He patted her hand and then leaned over again to dab her forehead with the cool damp cloth.

Despite the pain rampaging inside her, she smiled. Several minutes passed during which she stared into his eyes, almost losing herself in them. She felt that as long as she was looking into them, she'd be protected.

When she finally whispered to him that he could leave, Peter slid off the bedside chair and quickly returned with a nurse, who was already paging the doctor.

The next day, Shadow woke up feeling almost as confused as she had felt when she'd first regained consciousness. She knew now that what had happened to her—being attacked and shot by Crowe—had been real and not some horrible nightmare.

As she waited for the counselor who was supposed to help her "deal with" Crowe's assault, a painful fear burrowed inside her, like a pack of rats gnawing her flesh from the inside out. In an effort not to panic, she forced herself to concentrate on the tree outside her hospital room window. She watched its leaves dance, their tops rich green, their bottoms silver, the contrasting colors forming shifting patterns in the breeze.

IA Moore

The counselor, a red-haired man in his thirties, arrived at around eleven that morning. After introducing himself as David Hartley, and engaging her in some small talk, he asked Shadow how she felt about the assault she'd recently suffered. She told him she was still jumpy and afraid even though she knew she was safe in the hospital. She said that even knowing she was safe, she didn't *feel* safe. The counselor told her he would teach her some tools she could use to help control the fear. He promised to return every weekday.

A week later, after several visits by the counselor and by Peter, and an unpleasant visit from the police, she was beginning to feel somewhat better. The counselor arrived as usual, at eleven.

"How are you feeling today?" he asked.

"I'm all right. I'm still sore from where I was shot, and all around that area."

"How is the fear?"

"It's still there," she said. "I panic every time I hear my door open."

"Let me take you through a little exercise. Remember what we did yesterday? The relaxing your body from head-to-toe exercise? You said it helped a little?"

"Yes, it did," she replied.

He turned and switched on the tape player he'd brought. Gentle music drifted from it. It reminded her of

Racing Shadows

the sound of the breeze playing in the tree outside the window.

"I want you to start with that exercise, and once your body feels totally relaxed, we'll start with a second exercise. You let me know when you're feeling totally relaxed."

A few minutes later she said, "I feel relaxed."

"Today," he said, "I'm going to teach you how to relax your mind. Close your eyes now, Shadow. Then take a deep breath and hold it. Slowly let your breath out. Feel relaxation flow in as the air flows out. Nothing harmful will happen to you. You're safe here, Shadow. And your baby is safe."

It had surprised her the first time he'd mentioned her pregnancy, but she vaguely remembered having signed something giving him permission to access her medical records. He mentioned it daily, even though they hadn't yet spoken of it specifically.

"You've been through a lot though, Shadow. You need to learn to relax, for the health of yourself and of your baby. I'm going to help you do that now. Just concentrate on my voice and all that I describe. Picture yourself in a beautiful place, a place you'd like to go. Go there in your mind now. Go to this safe place where you're free and you can truly relax...."

In response, Shadow imagined herself in a field of blue flowers, lying on the grass, amidst the cool fragrance of the flowers. Around her moved horses, many beautiful horses, circling around...

When they finished, David told her to practice the exercise at least twice every day, and assured her that every time she did, she would begin to feel calmer. Every day she would feel stronger.

Peter visited her that evening. He sat at her bedside reading her *The Racing Form,* as he usually did. What else?

"I'm tired of that stuff," she said to him irritably. Even though her internal pain was lessening, she itched like mad under her bandages.

"What should I read you, then?" he asked her. "It's all I have here." He held up his empty palms.

"I don't know. I'm sick. Find something." She knew she was being difficult, but she also knew by now that Peter wouldn't abandon her because of it.

"Hmmm," he said, "I can pick up something tomorrow. Do you like romances?"

"No!"

"Westerns?" he asked, grinning now.

"Even worse."

"How about a mystery?"

"No," she sighed. "Not that either."

"Well, what then?"

"Tell me a story instead," she ordered.

"I don't know any stories."

"Of course you do," she said, smiling at him now. "And if you don't—just make one up."

There were a few seconds of silence.

Racing Shadows

"Well?" she looked into his eyes and at his smiling face. Behind him the leaves of her tree danced in the wind.

His expression cheerful and untroubled, he began, "Once upon a time, there was a little girl. Now, she was really a princess, but she didn't know this. She lived in the middle of the forest on a mountainside in a country near—"

"Peter," she said, interrupting him and picking up a red leather pouch from her bedside table. "Tell me about this again, will you? What's it for? When you first brought it, I was still kind of out-of-it."

He looked at her and grinned. "Was my princess story really that dull?"

She nodded. "Tell me about this pouch thing, again, please. I kind of remember, but I need you to tell me again. So I have it straight in my mind."

Peter reached out and touched the pouch, his fingers brushing hers. He touched her in some small way every time he came. It made her feel cared for.

"That's the pouch I brought for you from Billie. He asked me to give it to you. His sister made it especially for you. It's a medicine pouch. It contains magic herbs that she says will help you heal."

"Help me heal?"

"That's what Billie said."

"And by Billie's sister you mean ... Crowe's mother."

"Right. She and Billie feel devastated about what happened."

"Do you?" she asked.

He looked at her with narrowed eyes, as if she really had to ask. "Of course I do."

She sighed. "Don't." Then she wrung her hands, forcing herself, for the first time to ask about her attacker. "So where's Crowe?"

"He's in prison. And he's been permanently ruled off the track."

"I should hope so," Shadow huffed.

Peter went on to tell her about Crowe's arrest. Of course, Crowe claimed the gun going off had been an accident, that Shadow had attacked him first and that he had only been defending himself. He said that if he hadn't grabbed the gun from her, she would have shot and killed him.

"What a liar! That makes me so mad!" she said.

"Nobody believes his story, Shadow. Not to mention that I was there. I saw it happen. I only wish I could have stopped it." He frowned. "But it went so fast, all I was able to do was grab the gun out of his hand to prevent him from firing it a second time. I screamed for someone to call an ambulance as I held you, trying to staunch your bleeding."

She shook her head as he spoke. "It's lucky you were there. Or he'd probably *have* shot me a few more times."

"Don't worry. He's locked away where he can't reach you."

"Well, that's a relief." She sighed deeply. "I feel bad that he's in jail, but I think he's dangerous and

Racing Shadows

needs to stay there at least until he gets help for his anger and his drinking problem."

"Most people in your position would just wish him dead. He almost killed you."

She looked away from him, a tear gathering in the corner of her eye.

He reached over and took her hand in his. "I'm sorry. I shouldn't have said that. You should not have to think about that right now. Your job here is to rest and to heal."

She smiled at him, enjoying the touch of his hand in hers. "It's okay. The counselor who comes and talks to me is helping me deal with what happened to me."

She left it at that for now. In actuality, along with David helping her deal with what happened with Crowe, he was now also helping her come to grips with her past.

CHAPTER 8

Whenever Peter left, Shadow felt a void, a strange emptiness. And it never really went away until he returned.

Although David tried his best to help her, Peter's mere presence sometimes felt more healing than all of David's psychology. She knew that David was trying his best to help her come to grips with what had happened, both with the recent attack by Crowe and also the past violence she had suffered.

And David's treatments *were* helping her to remember her past more clearly. He and she spoke about the flash backs she'd been having of the young girl being abused. David told her that to get well, she'd have to sort out her memories. She'd have to sort out who the little girl in the flashbacks was. He explained that he thought that, very likely, the girl in the flashbacks was her younger self.

He explained that to heal emotionally, she needed to confront the origins of the flashbacks and figure them out, as they were likely partial memories of events she hadn't been able to face at the time they'd happened to her. He assured her that she now had a chance to fully remember from a *safe place*, the experiences and feelings that had been imploding on her current life. He promised to come any time, day or night, that she called for him.

She told him about her dream of the amber girl playing in the river. He asked her if she had any idea what the dream meant. She shook her head.

"How did you feel when you had the dream?" he asked.

"Frightened … and ashamed," Shadow admitted.

"Do you know who the man was?"

"No," she said, but she did. The man was Tony.

He asked her if she thought the dream was about herself as the little girl in the water. She said she wasn't sure. He asked if, alternatively, it could mean that she was fearful of what might happen to her own child one day.

"Maybe," she replied.

Then he asked if she wanted her baby to be a boy or a girl.

Immediately, she said, "A boy."

He asked her, "Why? Is there something bad that happens to girls?"

Shadow started to laugh, the answer was so obvious. He should have been embarrassed for asking it. She told him she didn't want to discuss the baby with him any longer.

He agreed not to bring the subject up. But he told her that she needed, ideally sometime before the birth, to decide whether or not to keep her baby or give it up for adoption.

Again, she said she didn't know, and began to panic.

David patiently took her through the exercise that calmed her down. Once she had relaxed, he assured her that talking to him would help her face both her past and current traumas and deal with them. And that, in turn, would help her to decide if she was prepared to keep the baby or not. He told her over and over that she was safe now, and that her baby was safe now. He told her to relax. "Relax. For your own good and for the sake of the baby."

And so she tried again, closing her eyes and going back to her blue-flowered field, the horses grazing so contentedly around her….

When she came back to herself, she began to cry and tried to sit up.

David took her hand in his. "It's all right, Shadow. You're safe now."

CHAPTER 9

"What is it! What's the surprise?" Shadow demanded. Peter had told her that he had a surprise for her, but refused to give it to her until she allowed him to kiss her. They'd been arguing the issue since he'd come into her hospital room several minutes earlier.

He shook his head. "No kiss, no surprise."

She studied him coldly, then turned away from him.

"A surprise for a kiss," he taunted.

"Go away!" she told him and started to sniffle.

"Hey, stop that. I'm only joking," he admitted.

She turned toward him again, but with a glare.

"I'm sorry for teasing you. The truth is, when you told me to come back with a story to tell you, I thought back to all of the stories I'd heard in my childhood and remembered the Grim Brothers', *Frog Prince*."

"And?" she asked.

He shrugged. "And it reminded me of you."

She tilted her head and smiled, now eager to hear what he was talking about. "A fairy tale?"

He nodded.

"Well, tell me then," she said, intrigued. "What's it about?"

"Well. A long time ago in a country far away, there lived a princess."

"I hope she's more interesting than the last one."

He ignored her comment. "She is very beautiful and the apple of the entire castle's eye. One sunny day, the princess is playing with a golden ball that rolls into a well.

"She runs to the edge of the well, bends over the rim, and lo and behold, she sees her ball.

"But an ugly green frog has it. She asks the frog to give it to her. He says he will if she'll promise to feed him, take him to her bed, and kiss him goodnight. She promises, but once she has her ball back, she forgets the promise and runs away with her ball.

"Later, her father finds out from one of the servants what his daughter has done and orders her to keep her promise. Reluctantly, the princess takes the creature to her room and feeds it, but when the frog demands to be placed in her bed and kissed, she disobeys her father, hurling it at the wall. This releases the frog from an evil spell and he turns into his rightful form—a prince."

"The princess's anger does that?" Shadow asked him.

He nodded.

She reached toward him, placing her palm against his cheek. Slowly, she brought her face closer to his and pressed her mouth gently on his lips. His eyes closed.

Racing Shadows

"Now I want my surprise!" she said, breaking the kiss. Had she not done so, she feared the chaste kiss would've turned into more than she'd intended.

During the kiss Peter hadn't moved a hair's breadth. It was almost as if, instinctively, he understood what she was just beginning to come to grips with herself— her fear.

He smiled.

"Well?" she prodded, "what's the surprise?"

"It's also a story."

"Really?" she asked. "Another one?"

"Yes. You said you wanted to hear one."

"I liked the frog one," she said, "but I'd love to hear another."

"This one is actually from Billie. He told it to me to tell to you."

"Well ... tell, then. I'm ready." She shifted in her bed, getting as comfortable as she could.

"Billie said that long ago, in the village of his people, there was a girl who loved horses."

She snuggled further down, under the covers, because the story sounded good already.

"The girl looked after all the braves' horses, leading them to the stream to drink and finding them the best and most tender shoots of grass to eat. She spoke softly to them and they followed her everywhere.

"The other girls noticed that the horses loved her and were jealous. They stopped speaking to her and so she spent more and more of her time alone with the horses, brushing them and healing their wounds when they were hurt.

"The girl spent her days with her mother, helping with the cooking and taking care of her little brother. But she longed to be with the horses and, as soon as she could, she slipped away from the tepee to be with them.

"The girl's life was very happy and very full until one day her father told her that it was time for her to marry. She did what her father bid and soon began a new life in her husband's tepee. She missed her mother and little brother, but even more, she missed the horses because her new husband would not allow her to be with them. He said they made her smell like one of them, an odor he didn't care for.

"One summer day, when the sun beat down on her, the girl felt very hot. She wandered down to the stream. There she spread her blanket in the meadow beside the water and lay down on it. The meadow was filled with white flowers and the breeze that blew over them carried their delicate scent. The chirping of the crickets lulled her and she fell asleep. Before long, the horses gathered around her and, in her sleep, she heard them moving about, neighing and chewing on the grasses."

Shadow's heart quickened. The story reminded her of her own special place, the meadow of blue flowers and her horses gathering round her.

"Footsteps approached her, but she did not wake. She smiled in her sleep, knowing somehow that she was back with the horses she loved. Suddenly, a hand gripped her wrist and yanked her to her feet. It was her husband and he was very angry.

"'I told you to stay away from the horses,' he said. 'I'm sorry,' she replied. 'They came to me while I was sleeping.'

"Her husband bent down and picked up a rock, throwing it at the nearest horse, hitting it in the side. Then he picked up another and another and threw them at the horses as they ran away. The girl began to cry and begged him to stop. He grabbed her harshly and took her back to their tepee, once more making her promise to stay away from the horses.

"She could not sleep that night, though, worrying about them. When she was sure that her husband was asleep, she crept out of the tepee and walked back toward the stream. In the meantime, the night had turned wild. Thunder rumbled in the sky and lightning flashed across the horizon.

"Suddenly, one of the horses appeared. It reared up in the air, frightened by the storm. She tried to speak to it and calm it down, but it was snorting and terrified, the whites of its eyes rolling about in its head, its mouth gaping wide open. Just then came the loudest clap of thunder she had ever heard. The girl grasped the horse's mane and swung herself onto its back. It reared again, screaming into the wind and began to run away, with her clinging on for her life."

"Bad idea," Shadow said, interrupting Peter. She was enjoying the story but felt anxious that the girl might perish, and didn't know if she wanted to hear the rest.

"How so?" Peter asked.

"Out west, they found a girl sitting on a horse. The two were dead. They'd been struck by lightning."

"And she was still sitting on him?"

"The paper said he was leaning against a mountain," she explained.

"How can a horse lean against a mountain?"

"I have no idea. Ask the *Edmonton Journal*."

He paused and looked at her, tilting his head. "Don't you like the story? Do you want me to stop?"

She shrugged. "It depends."

"On what?"

She wrung her hands together in her lap, feeling silly. "Is … Is the girl going to die?"

"No." He shook his head.

She took a deep breath and let it out slowly. "Then, I like it," she said. "Go on."

He raised a finger as if remembering something. "Oh. I forgot. Jessie said to ask you if you'd like to see someone named Paul."

She shook her head, her long dark hair falling partially over her eyes. "I only want to see you." Then she bowed her head in embarrassment at what she'd said, peeking at him through her lashes. His lips had curved up and his cheeks dimpled. She loved his smile.

He cleared his throat. "I'll continue the story then?"

She nodded. "Please."

Racing Shadows

"The horse galloped with the girl clinging to his back, farther and farther from her tribe and her husband. She could not stop the horse, nor did she want to. She held his long black mane between her fingers as her legs clasped his sides so tightly that she could feel his heart pounding though them.

"The horse ran farther and farther, the wind and the rain pelting him and the girl. She knew she should be afraid, that she should jump off him and try to find her way back to her people, yet she did not want to. She wanted to stay on the horse and race the wild storm.

"At last, the horse reached the rest of the herd. The girl slid from his back and moved from horse to horse, greeting each one. She was so happy to be with her horses again. Eventually, the rain stopped and the moon shone on her and the horses, their slick wet backs, their alert ears. The girl led the horses to a copse of woods where they lay down and rested, awaiting the morning sun."

"Did I ever tell you I was sorry?" she asked suddenly.

Peter stopped talking and smiled at her. "For what?"

"Getting mad at you. In the stall."

"You don't have to apologize."

"I wanted to hurt you," she admitted.

He sat quietly. "Perhaps I was your *Frog Prince*?" he asked.

His analogy didn't ease her guilt. "You didn't do anything wrong—and I wanted to hurt you!"

"But you didn't hurt me."

"You stopped me," she insisted.

He shook his head. "How so?"

She shrugged. She didn't know how he had stopped her. She searched his eyes for answers. He seemed so much wiser than she was. "I'm sorry," she finally said. "For everything. It wasn't really you I was mad at."

"Who were you mad at?" he asked.

She could only shake her head. For several minutes, they both remained silent.

"Do you think you could ever love me?" she asked, then put a hand to her mouth, aghast at her own words.

He stared at her, speechless, as though she were a little girl who had just asked him, although she was old enough to know better, if the tooth fairy really existed. He began to speak, then stopped, as though the question were too weighty.

"And then?" she asked, to break the silence and keep at least a shred of her dignity. "What happened in the morning?"

He gazed into her eyes for a long while, making her wish she'd kept her foolish question to herself. What must he think of her?

Finally, he continued with the story. "And, in the morning, she was awakened by the horse nuzzling her neck."

Shadow sighed. She loved the sound of Peter's voice.

"She could see the horse clearly now in the morning sunlight. He was white, but spotted with black, and he was a stallion. He pranced in front of the girl, as though

Racing Shadows

he wanted her attention. She remained sitting in the grass, just admiring his beauty. He pranced one way and then the other, growing more frantic, until finally she got to her feet and followed him. He led her among and through the herd of horses to a pure white foal. She gasped when she saw that the foal's eye had been put out, likely by one of the rocks that her husband had thrown. She caressed the lovely foal's neck and kissed its forehead. Tears fell from her eyes onto the foal until, as if by a miracle, the wound was healed and the eye was restored to its original brilliance. The painted stallion neighed with joy and the foal's mother approached the girl, encircling her with her long neck, in the only way that a horse can hug a human.

"The stallion neighed. The band of horses began to walk away, and again the stallion pranced, this time swinging his head around and pointing his nose at his back. She understood that he wanted her to ride him, so again she grasped a handful of his mane and swung onto him."

Shadow began to drift away, the sound of Peter's voice talking to her so soothing she closed her eyes.

The amber girl is in the shower, enjoying the warm water so much she doesn't want to get out. She stays in until, eventually, the water runs cold and she pulls back the curtain to step out.

A man is standing there, as if he'd been waiting. "You look frozen," he says, and Shadow struggles to look closer. She knows that it's important. She must figure out who these people are.

Suddenly she realizes: the amber girl is Shadow, herself, and the man is Tony!

Tony puts his hand on Shadow's bare shoulder as she steps out of the shower.

Shadow moans in pain as her flesh beneath his touch begins to burn. Like water on dry ice, heavy billows of steam roll down in grey waves to her feet, the cloud so thick that it covers her and she drops the towel she was wrapped in to the ground.

"Shadow," Peter said. "Shadow?"

Shadow jumped. She'd been completely immersed in the memory that had suddenly assaulted her.

"I'm sorry," she stammered. "I just … I just remembered something." Finally, she was beginning to understand the things that she had been keeping at bay. She was beginning to remember it all.

"Do you want me to go on with the story?" Peter asked.

"Yes. Please."

He cleared his throat and began again. "The people searched everywhere for the girl and the vanished horses. They were nowhere to be found.

"The girl decided to live with the horses. She didn't wish to return to the tribe and face her husband, who she knew would be furious with both her and the horses. The horses spent their days in meadows, eating lush grass while she rode on the stallion's back. The girl found plants and fruits to eat, berries, and sometimes honey. She was very happy.

"Then one day several weeks later, men from her village appeared on horseback. They called out to her. She quickly jumped onto the stallion's back and they fled, the herd following them far beyond where the braves could reach them. Her stallion was that swift.

"Once they had escaped the braves, however, the girl began to think about her mother and her little brother and became saddened. She no longer reveled in the freedom of her circumstances. Guilt plagued her and she could no longer enjoy her life among the horses.

"The stallion sensed that the girl was sad. He asked her what was wrong. She told him that she missed her tribe. He heaved a huge sigh. 'Will you take me back?' she asked him, for she knew that she could never find the way herself. 'Yes,' he said.

"The herd traveled for two days, and then, on the third day, she saw in the distance the stream and the tepees beyond. Her heart was overjoyed."

Shadow interrupted Peter. "I suppose you know that I'm pregnant," she said matter-of-factly, although her heart was racing and her hands trembling.

He looked at her and narrowed his eyes, as if assessing the truth of her statement. "No," he said carefully. "I did not know that."

"Well?" she said, her fists clenched.

He shrugged. "Well, what can I say? Congratulations."

She began to cry. "I wish she'd have killed me. I really do. Why didn't she just get rid of me and I wouldn't have had to go through all this."

Peter sat up taller and leaned toward her, looking concerned. "I don't understand. You wish who'd have killed you?"

"My mother," she said and sobbed.

"Your mother?" he repeated.

"Instead of having me and just throwing me away."

"Oh, I think I'm following you. Your mother gave you up for adoption? And you think she should have aborted you?"

"Yes!"

"Having an abortion would have been easier for her, I suppose," he said.

"Really? I think it would have been easier to have me and give me away. She could pretend I was going to some wonderful home. Then she wouldn't have a thing to feel guilty about. Not like if she'd killed me."

"That is one way of looking at it." He smiled at her. "We won a race today."

She clenched her teeth. How could he think about races when she was telling him about her deepest, most painful secrets? "I almost wish I'd aborted this baby. I just couldn't force myself to." Peter was the first person she'd told this to.

Peter looked at her as if she'd slapped him. "Why?" he finally asked.

"Because I don't want a baby."

Racing Shadows

"The way your mother didn't want you?" he asked. "You don't know she didn't want you, Shadow. Your mother might have wanted you very much, just hadn't been able to keep you."

"Well, I don't want my baby to be born just to suffer."

"You don't know that your baby would suffer," he said.

She shrugged. "I really don't know what to do now. Do I keep it or surrender it for adoption?" She shook her head and looked down.

"Hey, Shadow," he said and she lifted her head. "Don't think you're alone in all this. I will support whatever you decide to do. I'll be here to help you. As long as you will let me do that."

"I should have aborted it. It's just some cells. It's part of my body!" she said with emphasis.

"Some people think that, for sure," he said. "But you don't have to listen to them. There are people who feel an unborn baby is its own person, not a part of its mother's body. Plus, having an abortion is illegal."

"Are you trying to guilt trip me?" she asked.

Peter was quiet for a while. "Not at all. I'm saying I think you made the right decision. Truthfully, whichever decision you'd made, it would be the right decision for you."

She felt a chill run through her, and knew he was right. It was her decision. And there was still one more to make. She was glad she'd told Peter. Putting it out in the open had helped. She was surprised he hadn't asked about the father.

He took a deep breath and smiled, but Shadow didn't want to think about reality right then. She wanted to hear more of Peter's story. "Can you tell me more of the story?"

"Of course," he said.

"The girl was glad to be home and couldn't wait to see her mother and brother. But before she knew it, there was her husband, striding toward them.

"'Come here,' he commanded. She stayed astride the horse. Her husband bolted to the stallion, grabbed her, and pulled her down off his back. Then he picked her up in his arms and carried her back to their tepee.

"Much to the girl's horror, he would not let her see her mother or brother, but instead, kept her confined to the tepee.

"The stallion was sad. He missed the girl and neighed longingly for her in the night. Time passed. Days and weeks. The girl was sad and the stallion was sad. Soon it would be winter and the snow would fly.

"One night, when the stallion was calling her, the girl slipped out of the tepee and ran to him. So happy was she to see him, she threw her arms around his neck and kissed him. Suddenly, before her stood not a horse, but the strongest, tallest brave she had ever seen. She gasped in wonder.

"'Your love for me turned me into a human,' he said. 'Now we can be together forever.' As she fell into

Racing Shadows

his arms, a noise in the brush startled her. Her husband had awoken and found them. His roar was like that of a bear's.

"Suddenly, the man in her arms turned back into a stallion and stood on his hind legs. He struck out, and a single blow from his front hoof felled her husband dead. Then, just as suddenly, the stallion turned back into a brave.

"The girl was welcomed back to the village with the strange brave. No one was upset about the death of her husband because he had never been well-liked in the tribe. They had all blamed him for the loss of their herd of horses. They felt it only right that he had been killed by one of the horses he loved to torment.

"The girl and the brave married and lived happily ever after in the village, both taking tender care of their herd of horses."

"The end," Peter pronounced.

"That was so beautiful," Shadow said, goose bumps prickling the skin of her arms, making the fine hairs stand up straight.

"Happily ever after always is." Peter smiled at her.

She sighed deeply. "I had a dream. About a girl. Do you believe in dreams?"

"Do you mean a hope kind of dream, or a dream you have when you're sleeping?"

"A night dream. Do you believe in those?"

"You mean do I believe they mean something, or that they come true?"

"Yes."
"Which?"
"Both."
"I don't think they necessarily come true."
"Oh?" She folded her arms across her chest and closed her eyes. What she really wanted was to look at him, deep into his eyes. She wanted to talk to him and tell him everything about her past that she could remember. But she didn't dare to. Instead, she pretended to fall asleep.

After a few minutes, she heard Peter get out of his chair and leave, his footsteps echoing across the tile floor. She wondered if he'd been waiting for that moment, just waiting for the opportunity to leave. He had on his suit again. She wondered where he was going. Suddenly, she felt guilty for taking up so much of his time—she wasn't his responsibility.

She decided that as soon as she saw a nurse, she'd tell her not to let visitors in to see her for the next day or so. She didn't want or need anyone's pity. All she needed was to remember all the fragmented pieces of her past and put them together in a story that made sense. Figure out exactly what happened and why it did. Only once she'd done that could she make her decision about the baby.

She squeezed her eyes shut in an effort to force herself to remember.

Racing Shadows

The heavy billows of steam encompass the two of them as Tony leads her toward the bed.
Shadow feels his hands crawling all over her, his fingers like huge spider legs touching every part of her body—hers, not his, he has no right. She is repulsed, but she can't scream. She can't stop what's happening.

Shadow gasped for air. Suddenly there wasn't enough in the room. The memory—was it real? If so, she couldn't bear it! She wanted to scream, to run, to throw herself out the window! Had she not remembered David's coaching, perhaps she would've. Instead of screaming and running, she closed her eyes, reached to her night table for the red medicine pouch and clasped it fiercely in her hand, as though it held the answers to all the mysteries of the world. Then she concentrated as hard as she could on her field of blue flowers. She slowed her breathing, inhaling the scent of the flowering grasses, the sun warm on her face, and the horses shifting and milling about....

CHAPTER 10

Shadow dreams the sea: she and Peter in the sea, floating about, immersed in ocean water. Breathing in the water as though it were air, Shadow sees that they are not alone. They are surrounded by thousands of creatures: fish, sea horses, starfish, and dolphins swim with them.

Shadow is filled with bliss. She wants to remain in the sea with Peter forever. Until eventually, she tires, grows so weary that she has to sleep, even though she doesn't want to and, helpless to stop herself, she slips down through the water to the bottomless bottom….

When Shadow awoke, she was crying and David was at her side.

"What happened? What were you dreaming about?" He handed her a tissue.

Shadow sniffed into her tissue, then straightened up in her bed. She told him her dream. "But it wasn't scary or anything—I have no idea why it made me cry."

"Maybe because you slipped away from Peter? Or because you slipped to the bottomless bottom, as you put it. Which is frightening, or at least it would be to me." He shrugged.

"What did the ocean and creatures mean?"

"I can't tell you for sure, but there are theories interpreting dreams of water and fish. Water can symbolize the psychic world, emotions, and intuition. Fish and other sea creatures swimming in water can mean that your dream is highlighting feelings you haven't yet consciously recognized. People swimming down deep in the water can represent peril.

"Maybe it means I was afraid of losing myself," she said in a quiet voice. She looked down at her hands, her fingers grasping the pale blue blanket.

A warm palm cupped her chin. "Look at me," David said.

She did.

"Relax. You are safe now. No one will hurt you."

She nodded.

"Do you feel safe?"

"Yes," she said. "I feel safe."

"Listen to me."

She closed her eyes.

"What you know is in layers. What you feel is in layers. You are only brushing at the edges of your feelings, your knowledge. Go deeper. Deeper. Go down into the water. Go back to what really was. Go back to your past."

IA Moore

Shadow hears her bedroom door opening and whirls around to see who's there. She freezes when she sees it's Tony.

He approaches her and she wants to run, but she can't move. At first, he doesn't say a word. Instead, he pulls her to him as he opens his robe. He presses her face into his shoulder, then down to his chest and even lower. "Kiss me," he orders. "Do it!" At first she tries, but then she sickens and starts to retch. She tries to pull away from him but he grabs her shoulders. Then he wraps his big hands around her throat and squeezes until she can't breathe and begins to collapse.

Then everything goes black, until suddenly she is watching the scene from above. Standing over her, Tony fumbles with her clothing. All she can see now is his dark shape on top of her. She is lost in the folds of his dark robe. Seconds pass. Then minutes. It feels like hours until he walks away, leaving her lying on the floor. She can hear herself cry. She is crying and coughing and retching and bleeding.

Finally she gets up, stumbles to the bathroom and climbs into the shower to wash away the blood, wash away his touch, wash away everything. She scrubs and scrubs and scrubs until her skin is red and raw. Then she lies there, in the bottom of the shower, crying and shaking.

When she came back to her senses, Shadow realized that David was there with her. *What?* Then she

Racing Shadows

remembered him telling her to go back to her past. It had worked.

Slowly she described to him all that she'd recalled.

"First I was simply *in* the scene. Then suddenly, I was above everything looking down on myself and Tony as if I were watching a movie of us."

"You were re-living a memory in the form of a flashback. Think back to it now. Try and picture it in your mind as an actual memory."

She thought back, managing to switch the scene from a flashback to a memory. "The part where I watched us from above was odd," she said. "Right before it, he choked me until I passed out. So the part where I was watching us from above must have been my imagination?"

"I believe so. It was your imagination filling in what you thought was happening while you were either semi-conscious or totally unconscious."

"So all of the flashbacks were real events you think? And the little girl was me too."

He nodded. "Yes, they were real and were you."

"Why didn't I just remember this stuff happening to me, not see it in these weird flashes?"

"Deep down you didn't want to know. You didn't want to face the fact that it was you being abused and you helpless to stop the abuse. So you imagined somebody else, a stranger, the one you called the amber girl, in your place. And now finally, the stranger has turned into you."

"So the amber girl wasn't real at all?"

"She was very real—she was you!"

Shadow thought back, concentrating, and realized what he'd said was true. "So this amber girl/woman … is like … my other personality?"

"In a sense, yes. She came out when you were in a situation you couldn't face being in. She's not an entire personality, though, as in multiple identity disorder. And now that you know what was going on, I think you are on the road to recovering your memories. The next time that you have a flashback, if I'm not with you at the time, focus on recalling the memory behind the flashback. Our final goal is for you to recall your past at will, without being triggered by a flashback. Then the flashbacks themselves will disappear." He smiled at her. "Good work today. You should rest now."

Then he got up and walked away, closing the door to her room. Leaving her trembling. She was too proud to call him back.

CHAPTER 11

The next day she spent alone. Peter didn't visit. No one came. She missed seeing Peter.

Even though Shadow tried to relax, questions kept popping into her head. She wondered who was paying for her hospital room. Who was paying for the counselor. Or maybe it was all free. Maybe she was some kind of rare and prized specimen: an A-1-Top-Class-Schizo-Loonie. Maybe David was planning to present a paper on her. Maybe he wanted to make his mark in the field of Loonieology. She shook her head. Putting herself down by telling herself stupid jokes wasn't cutting it.

She sighed. She knew she should be grateful for the free bed and board and treatments. And she was, but more than anything else, she wanted to get out of the hospital. She wanted to go home. But where? Where was her home? How could she have allowed this situation to happen: Pregnant with her foster father's baby? She began to sob, then shook her head in disgust. No use feeling sorry for herself. She truly was lucky to be here, protected. After all, it could have been worse. At least she was free of Tony.

The worst thing was that she couldn't help wondering if she'd let it all happen on purpose. Did she just replay her birth mother's script? Unwanted pregnancy, unwanted baby, unwanted child. Child free for the taking in any which way anyone wanted her. Did she subconsciously orchestrate the sad tale all over again. If so, why? For whom?

Shadow closed her eyes and focused. She had to sort the situation out. She needed to understand her motives. David said that she'd been unable to face what was happening, so she invented another persona—the one she called the amber girl to stand in for her and go through the hell she herself couldn't face. Was that true? All she knew was that her life had come tumbling down like a child's too-tall block tower.

Picking up the pouch, she closed her eyes and drifted back to her field of flowers and horses.

Peter returned the next day.

"The nurses said you weren't accepting visitors when I came yesterday and the day before," he said, as he sat in the chair by her bedside. "I've been worried ever since. Is anything wrong?"

She'd been waiting all day, unable to think about much except whether or not he'd show up. Now she was as pleased as the cat who swallowed the canary, the bear who found the honey, the—"I was just in a mood. I'm sorry," she replied. "I told the nurse to keep visitors away for a couple of days."

Racing Shadows

"Everyone gets to be in a mood sometimes," he said. "It's allowed." He paused. "Actually, I didn't know if I should come back today but I thought I'd try."

"Are you mad you came for nothing yesterday and the day before?" she asked. Beneath her folded arms, she was trembling. *Please say no*, she said inside her head.

"No. Not at all."

"Did you miss me?" she asked then, catching her lower lip with her front teeth, and regretting the question as soon as it left her lips.

He smiled. "Yes."

A wash of relief swept over her. "I missed you."

He reached across the bedcovers and took her hand, squeezed it lightly, then let it go.

Her heart raced, and she was afraid to speak, scared she might say something stupid like, *I love you*. They sat in silence for several minutes, just smiling at each other.

"Are your parents still alive?" she finally asked him.

He nodded.

"Do you ever see them or the rest of your family?"

"My mother and father only had one kid—me. And from the time I was about six, I lived with my aunt, who adopted me. I don't know how well my parents even remember me. I write sometimes. Cards, you know…"

"Aren't you ever lonely?"

He shrugged. "Not really."

"Well, do you see your aunt?"

"I did, until she died. She was quite a bit older than my mother. She died of a stroke."

"I'm sorry."

He was silent for a while, lost in thought it appeared. She waited for him to say something.

"What are you going to do now?" he asked her.

"What do you mean?"

"Is there someone you want to contact? I know you didn't drop out of the sky. I know you have people someplace. Your baby has a father." He gave her a probing look, his eyebrows raised.

"Sort of…"

"Are you … um … married?" he asked with some hesitancy.

She shook her head. "No. Are you?"

He threw back his head and laughed.

"It's not that funny," she said.

He shrugged. "I'm a dwarf. My own parents couldn't handle that. I'm just lucky some well-meaning tall person hasn't euthanized me for my own good. I mean, there's even a song about it." He grinned and started to sing 'Short People.'"

"That was a lame song," she said, shaking her head. Then she looked into his eyes, "Where do you go?"

"What?"

"When you wear your suit, I mean. I thought … I thought you might be going somewhere special."

He studied her for a while, reached over and squeezed her hand again. "If I tell you, will you be mad?"

Racing Shadows

"No. Why would I be?" she asked, feeling herself tense, as if his answer might fracture her fragile persona.

He took a deep breath before speaking and let it out slowly. "I go to visit a friend, a woman who's small like me. She lives in a cottage on the lake. She cooks us dinner and then we watch TV." He shrugged. "Sometimes, we talk all night and I don't get back until morning."

"Oh, I thought it was something like that." She shut her eyes, but the tears leaked out anyway.

"What's wrong?" he asked.

"Nothing."

"Then why the tears?"

"I thought … I wanted … nothing!"

"You're mad at me. I knew it." he said, slapping his knee.

"I'm not mad," she insisted. There was a pause. "I'm jealous," she admitted.

"Of Marjorie? If I told her that, she'd fall on the floor laughing."

"That's just what I mean!"

"What?"

"You know each other. You're friends."

He nodded. "Yes, we are."

"Is that all?"

"Come on."

"Why can't I ask? You asked if I was married. And you saw her just a couple of nights ago."

He sighed. "How do you know?"

"The suit."

"She'd give anything to be like you," he said quietly. "To be strong and beautiful."

Shadow felt as though she'd been gut-punched and said nothing. Just let the guilt flow over her. Other people were always so much more together than she was. She was always so spoiled and ungrateful for the good things she had. She wished she could change and turn happy like everybody around her. "I'm not beautiful, you know," she finally said.

"What makes you think that?" he asked without sarcasm.

She shrugged. Did he really want to know? Couldn't he see? "Well," she began. "My color's too dark, my mouth's too big, my chin is cleft, I'm too skinny and…. And my legs are … weird," she finished without interest. She'd enumerated her failings many times, both physical and mental.

"I think you look like … Kiss. Yes, you look just like Kiss did. I'll bet you can run too."

Without wanting to, she smiled. "I used to like to run."

Again, he took her hand, rubbing his thumb across the top of it. "And you've got the softest skin I've ever felt."

"What does that matter?" she demanded, suddenly angry, no, scared, afraid at what he said about her skin … the way he looked at it. The way she felt when he said it.

Racing Shadows

"What's wrong?" he asked, putting down her hand and sitting back in the chair. "I didn't mean to upset you."

"No." She shook her head. "It wasn't that, it was just that … there's something wrong with me!" she blurted.

"What do you mean? What's wrong with you?"

Shadow looked at him, into his concerned green eyes. She knew what she wanted to tell him: how she felt dirty and guilty, and how she didn't think anyone would ever be able to look past her sins and love her. But she didn't. She told him something less damning, but equally true. "I mean I don't know why I'm here or who I am or where I belong," she said, a frown tugging at both corners of her mouth as she struggled against it. She didn't want to burst into tears.

"How old are you?" he asked.

She shrugged. "Nineteen."

He laughed. "You're not supposed to know that stuff yet. If you stop worrying about it, it'll all take care of itself."

"Well, how old are you?"

"Thirty-four."

"And what are you here for?"

"To enjoy life, basically."

She squinted at him. "Not to offend you but when someone says that, I usually think they mean they enjoy life by getting drunk and screwing around. Is that what you mean?"

He tilted his head, as though considering, a small grin on his bearded face. "I hardly ever drink," he said finally.

"Are you making fun of me?" she demanded.

"Maybe a little," he admitted.

"So then ... do you enjoy yourself with Marjorie?" Shadow asked.

"Yes, I do. And I enjoy myself at work and I ... it isn't... I enjoy many things in life. There are so many things to enjoy."

"Yes, yes. I know. You're talking about all the little things. Sunshine, enough food to eat, a roof over your head, yada yada. The thing is that a person with a past like mine is always too busy fighting some battle in their own minds to enjoy anything!" She sighed.

"You know what I think?"

"What do you think?" she asked.

"I think you should call your boyfriend or your family. I think you should go home." He gave her a stern look and she felt as though he'd just told her to "grow up."

He shifted in the chair.

"Are you leaving?" she asked. She felt panicky—she didn't want him to go yet. Should she ask him to stay? Sadly, she realized that it must be an effort for him to come here every night ... an inconvenience. She thought she was important because she'd been shot, that everyone would automatically want to care for and help her.

Racing Shadows

He got down from the chair. "It might be best. You need your rest."

"You don't have to come, you know," she said as coldly as she could. What she didn't say was: please stay, you're my only friend. "I'll be fine. The doctor said I'll be healed and out of here in a few weeks. Go someplace else."

"Don't you want to see me anymore?" he asked, a frown taking over his face.

"It doesn't matter to me." she said, then shrugged and turned her head away from him.

"You're sure?"

"I'm sure."

He sighed. "All right. If that's the way you want it. I guess I've been told."

"Bye," she said without turning her head to watch his retreat. That would be like torturing herself ... not to mention that she just might beg him to come back.

She heard the door shut and felt desperately empty. She'd miss him, he was her friend. She didn't care about Marjorie—didn't care if the woman got hurt or not.

That wasn't why she sent Peter away. She sensed he was attracted to her, felt something for her—she could see it in his eyes, feel it in the touch of his hand. Could it be that she was afraid? Afraid to get too close to him and, as a result, be hurt? She began to cry.

A week later, she felt stronger, felt as though she could finish what she and David had begun. Even though she was lonely without Peter's company, she decided that she'd made the right decision telling him not to come back. Without the distraction of him and her feelings for him, she could better concentrate on her counseling sessions. She needed to be alone and he did too, she told herself. Each of them needed some time and space to figure things out.

After drinking her breakfast juice, she began again the process of relaxation, the process of re-living those months and weeks and days before she came here. Every day, the counselor came and they talked things out—mostly the way she coped back then, the significance of those coping mechanisms, and how they related to her now, her confusion.

She squeezed the medicine pouch, lay down in her blue-flowering field, hearing the singing of birds and the graceful movements of her horses....

"Hi, Shadow."

She opened her eyes to see Paul.

"Hi," she said, trying to smile at him, hide her disappointment that he wasn't Peter. "What time is it?" she asked, yawning.

"Eight forty-five. We've only got fifteen minutes before visiting hours end."

Peter used to come at seven.

Racing Shadows

"Oh my gosh," she said. "I slept through supper." The tray holding her meal still sat on her bed table.

"You need your rest," Paul said. "I've never been shot myself, but I'm pretty darn sure that your body is doing a lot of work just healing itself. Not to mention your ... I mean," he finished, stuttering....

"My pregnancy, you mean. I know," she said. "Don't be embarrassed. It's no big secret anymore. And how are you? How's your mom?"

"Fine. She says hello. So do Jessie and Abby. And Georgia."

"Well, hello to them too," Shadow said.

There was a silence. Obviously Paul didn't know what to say when things weren't good; he only knew how to tease and flirt. But not with someone with an infected gun wound in her back. She was feeling too tired for small talk and the blipping noises the IV made non-stop were getting on her nerves.

Just to end the uncomfortable silence, she asked, mock-cheerfully, "So when's the big day?"

"Next December, when she gets laid off and I finish my exams."

"You're kidding me! You asked her again and this time she said yes?"

"That's right," he said, looking proud of himself.

"Honeymoon?"

"A week in Vegas."

Shadow laughed. "You're kidding me."

"Nope. She loves to gamble."

"Well, go to the Bahamas. They have casinos. And it's nicer. You can swim in the ocean. I've never even seen the ocean."

"It's what the lady wants." He shrugged.

"I guess it could be worse."

"Yeah, she could want Niagara Falls."

"Right," Shadow said and laughed.

He reached over and lifted her arm up off the blue blanket and studied it. "Hey, don't they feed you in here?" he asked. "You look like a skeleton. You must've lost twenty pounds."

"They feed me," she answered, pulling her arm away. "But how can a person work up an appetite lying in bed?"

"You really want me to answer that?"

She looked at him and groaned out loud, trying to frown. At least he wasn't treating her like an invalid any longer.

He grinned, looking pleased at having successfully teased her. Then he gave her a serious look, cleared his throat and asked, "Is someone coming to get you? To take you home?"

"Why does everyone ask me that?" she said in frustration. "No, no one's coming to get me. I don't *have* anyone to get me."

"Sorry," he said sheepishly. "But in that case, I wanted to ask you if you'd stay on at the house. We—I mean, me and my brothers and sisters—will pay you to keep an eye on our mother. We were planning to hire

Racing Shadows

someone this year as a companion. You'll be out of the hospital by September, won't you?"

She smiled. That was a life-saving offer if she'd ever heard one! If she decided to keep the baby, she wouldn't be able to work with horses while looking after a new-born. "Thanks, Paul. I'd really love that. I'd really be grateful."

"Good, then it's settled?"

"As long as it's all right that I might keep my baby."

"Well ... yes, of course. I had assumed you would be keeping it." He gave her a puzzled look but didn't say anything else.

"I'm due in late December, early January."

"Have you seen a doctor?"

"Just the doctor who is looking after me here. But they did an ultrasound and said everything looks fine. And I have the name of an obstetrician to see when I get out of hospital. Actually, I already have an appointment booked. So everything's good right now." Despite her assertion that everything was good, she felt anxiety wash over her—thinking about the baby did that to her. But now, at least she knew she had a place to stay. She knew she'd enjoy being a companion to Mrs. Shevchuk and was very grateful for Paul's offer. Maybe things could turn out well after all. "Look Paul," she said. "I'm very thankful for your offer. And I am really doing well right now. But, but I do need to sleep again."

"Sure." He looked at his watch. "It's just about time anyway. Have a good rest." He brushed her cheek with his lips. "Sleep tight."

"Thanks so much for coming," she said sleepily as he walked out. Then she adjusted her position, pulled the cord to turn off the light over her bed, and immediately fell asleep.

CHAPTER 12

After Paul left, she slept right through until a nurse woke her for breakfast: cornflakes and juice. Shortly after the nurse took away her tray, her doctor examined her. He was tall and older with a bushy grizzled moustache, and under his white lab coat, he wore a track suit. He also smelled nice and laughed easily.

Neither of which seemed to be helping her get better. Today, he told her she had a high temperature. Once they had established this fact—again—she was given the medicine necessary to drop her fever. Because of the baby, her medications had to be safe for pregnancy, which made curing her more difficult apparently, at least that's what the medical staff told her. She took the medication gratefully, like candy, and lay with her face turned to the window, waiting for the sun to rise. She still had to think through her past. Figure things out.

Maybe when she got out of the hospital, she'd understand everything better. Then she'd tell Peter about her past—the entire truth of it. That's what she wanted to do, but she was afraid of what he'd think: that she was ruined? Spoiled? He knew she was pregnant and unmarried, but he had no idea of ... the other things that had been done to her. She knew she wasn't normal. Could he understand?

Slipping into panic mode, she closed her eyes and tried to float back to her field of flowers and horses, clutching the medicine pouch in her hand. But she couldn't. Probably because she was still worrying about how Peter would feel about her if he knew the truth of her past. She sighed. Sometimes she just wanted to forget everything, lose the baby, and have her whole past go away with it. As soon as she had this thought, she broke down in tears. It was no solution.

She lay thinking about the baby and about her past. She recalled a young vet who had worked for Tony—the day the man had refused to go through with the spaying of a cat when he discovered she was already pregnant, because he just couldn't abort the unborn kits. He sewed her back up without changing a thing and Tony had had to open her again and take everything out—ovaries, womb, kittens. Tony had told the story at supper that night, unable to decide whether to remain furious about the inconvenience the incident had caused him or to be amused at the man's naiveté. Eventually, his sense of humor won over and he laughed. Shadow had said, "That's not funny!" got to her feet and left the room. Accustomed to her usual strict obedience and unquestioning respect, Tony made sure she paid for her remark.

Racing Shadows

And now *she* had had the power to destroy an unborn life and she hadn't done it. She went over her decision again, trying to determine if she'd done the right thing. When she imagined a new life, a real baby growing inside her, she was sure she'd made the right call. Still, she knew that in order to give the baby a good life, if she decided to keep it, she had to become a better person. The option of giving the baby up for adoption did not sit well with her, because ... because of Tony. She wouldn't condemn her child to suffer the pain that Tony had caused her, even if the chance of it happening was small. She had no control over what might happen to her child if it was placed with foster or adoptive parents. Her heart racing, she decided, then and there, to keep it, vowing to give her child the best life she could!

David would soon arrive. He seldom smiled. Perhaps he didn't think it appropriate, considering the state of her mind.

So when he walked into her room, she gave him a broad smile. He smiled back and she felt pleased. She wasn't sure how she felt about him—the way he seemed to accept her for what she was, the way he genuinely listened to her. He said she was a good patient: that she had the motivation to overcome her resistance to being cured. She'd almost laughed when he said that. To be cured of what, she wanted to ask, but felt too embarrassed. But really, what did she have? There had to be a diagnosis. She wished she could read his notes.

David had told her that once she'd re-lived everything, she'd have to deal with Tony somehow or he'd remain in her life.

"He is out of my life already," she'd replied.

"Your life here," he said, pointing at his head. "And here." He pointed to his heart.

She nodded, understanding his meaning. But what did David think he was—an exorcist? The thought made her smile.

She picked up the pouch and asked him to guide her through a memory. He floated her back to her safe meadow until the memories begin to seep in, coalescing on her nineteenth birthday, the day she had planned to tell Barbara about her pregnancy.

The day of Shadow's birthday, Barbara had presented her with the gift of a beautiful marble horse statue and prepared her favorite supper, roast chicken with mandarin dressing and potato salad.

That evening, Shadow stands in front of her foster parents in their living room as they sit, side-by-side, on a black couch. In an effort to stay calm, she looks above their heads at a large painting of a hunt scene with horses and hounds milling around, and a fox hiding behind a bush.

"Mom," she begins, sobbing, "I need to tell you about my ... my ... condition and how I think it must've happened."

Racing Shadows

Suddenly Tony leaps from the couch and grabs her arm. "Oh my God, I forgot," he says. "Shadow, I need your help at the barn. There's a colicking horse I need to check on." He looks at his watch. "I should have been there an hour ago!"

"How could you forget?" Barbara asks.

"The alarm I set didn't go off! Hurry up, Shadow!"

She is torn. Is the colicking horse just a story he's inventing to stop her from telling Barbara that she's pregnant, and that she believes it's with Tony's child? Has he anticipated what she was about to say? Or is there really a horse in need of medical attention? She debates it in her mind, then decides to err on the side of caution and go with him.

Sitting in the passenger seat of his SUV, she glances at him. His jaw is working, the muscles standing out. What is he worried about—the horse or what she'd been about to say? She doesn't know. She asks him a question about the sick horse, but he doesn't reply.

When he turns the car down a road that she knows doesn't lead to the barn, she realizes that there is no horse.

Her breathing speeds up. What will he do to her? Her heart pounds against the walls of her chest as if it wants to escape, and her mind races. What should she do? Open the door and throw herself out? They are traveling too fast for her to jump out of the car without being badly injured, but if he slows down to turn, should she attempt it? Or would it be better to try and convince him that she had been about to tell Barbara something totally different? But what? She racks her brain but comes up with nothing.

Suddenly the car slows and begins to turn down a path leading into the woods. In a determined burst of fear-fueled energy, she pushes open her door and launches herself out of the vehicle, rolling across the baked mud into the weeds and bushes growing alongside.

As she hears the car start to brake, she springs to her feet and runs into the woods, not stopping until she hasn't an ounce of breath left inside her. Diving behind the trunk of a large fallen tree, she tries to still her breathing enough to listen for him, to hear if he is still behind her.

She can hear him shouting, but his voice comes from a place far behind her—he must've given up the chase long before she stopped running. She can't make out exactly what he is saying, just the odd words like "kill" and "bitch".

Relief washes over her. She is sure that he won't pursue her further.

Once Shadow had re-lived the scene in her mind and returned to the present, and described it to David, he nodded and said, "You finally refused to be his victim. You'd had enough."

"Too bad it took me so long," she said, filled with shame.

Racing Shadows

"Don't blame yourself. It's quite understandable. He began abusing you when you were too small to fight him. Once someone exerts that kind of power and control over you, it's hard to get out of that mindset. He hit you, tormented you, molested and raped you, tortured and dominated you. You'd finally reached a point where you felt you were ready to expose him for the monster he was." He regarded her solemnly. "I'm proud of you. That took a great deal of courage."

"Do you think what I did got through to him?" she asked.

He nodded. "Yes. I think you got through to him that it wasn't happening anymore. Did you go back home after that? Did you go to the police?"

She shook her head. "I spent that night under the fallen tree. In the morning, when I knew he was at work, I went back home. Nobody was there. I grabbed a small suitcase, packed my wallet, savings, papers, and the birthday present Barbara had given me, and walked to the highway. Then I stuck out my thumb and hitched rides until I made it to the airport. I got on a plane and ended up in Toronto, then hitched rides to here. End of story."

"Or maybe the beginning of a much better one?" he asked, raising his eyebrows.

She laughed, pointed at herself lying in the hospital bed. "Better, yes, but if this is as good as it gets...."

He put his hand on hers. "Things will improve for you Shadow. Your body will heal and you will do the work you need to do to heal your mind."

Although she trusted David's words promising that her life would improve, for the time being she felt as limp and sad as an old, wet rag.

She wanted to believe that she could recover emotionally, and that she could give birth and be a good mother, but at the same time she realized how hard it would be. What would she tell her child when he or she asked where they came from, who their father was? How could she respond in a way that would spare her child from pain?

She thought about the book she'd used to read to the children she babysat from time to time, the book called *Where Is My Mother?* In the story, a little bird hatches alone, then walks around asking everyone and everything from a kitten to a bulldozer if they are his mother, until he finds her at the end. The children loved it. It had been their favorite.

The memory strengthened her resolve to keep her baby.

Her thoughts were interrupted when Billie Moon walked through her door. She was taken aback; she didn't know him very well, not to mention that it'd been his nephew who shot her. But … he did send her the medicine pouch, and through Peter, the story.

"Well, little girl, you're looking damn fine today," he said as he crossed the room to her bedside.

"Thank you, boss," she said.

"You can call me Billie." He took the chair beside her bed.

"Thanks for the medicine pouch."

"Don't mention it. I'm just very sorry for what happened. If I hadn't given you the job of waking him up, none of this would've happened." He shook his head, as if in disbelief at his stupidity.

"Crowe pretty much hated me at first sight ... so it might have gone down that way anyway."

"I knew he was lazy and drank too much, but I never knew he could be violent that way. Good God!"

She shrugged. "He claims it was an accident."

"Of course that's what he'd say. Peter told me exactly what happened though, and it was no accident."

She sighed. "Yeah. The main thing is that I am okay, and my baby's okay." By now she figured everyone had heard about her pregnancy.

"Congratulations, by the way," he said. "I'm sure you'll be a great mother. And anything that baby needs, I'm here for you."

A feeling of warmth ran through her at his offer. "Thank you very much. I really appreciate your help. By the way, that was a beautiful story you told Peter to tell me."

"You liked it?"

"Very much."

"You're Métis, right? Do you know the Indian side of your family?"

"Yes, I'm Métis, but no, I know nothing about either side of my family," she replied. "I think someone once told me that my mother was Cree. But that's all I know. I was brought up in foster care in a white family."

"Did you ever think you might want to discover your Indian heritage?"

She shrugged. "Not really."

"I understand that. But you may change your mind one day. I have relatives out west that could help you if you do decide differently in the future. Just let me know."

"Well, right now, I'm too mixed up in my head to even think about that."

"I understand," he said softly. Then, in a boisterous tone: "So when are you getting out of this dump and back to work?"

"Soon as they let me," she said, grinning. "I'm pretty sick of sitting around staring at these four walls. I'm literally chomping at the bit to get out of here."

"I wouldn't stay in a hospital if my life depended on it. At my age, once they got hold of me, they'd likely never let me out again." He laughed. "Our custom is to let family members take care of us if we get hurt or sick."

"That makes a lot of sense," she said.

"You think so?"

"Yeah."

"Then why won't you let Peter back here to take care of you?"

Goosebumps popped up all over her body at his words. "Did … did he say I wouldn't let him back?"

Racing Shadows

"Not in so many words."

"Actually, we both decided it'd be better if he didn't come." That was sort of the truth—when Shadow had asked Peter to stay away, he hadn't protested. "He doesn't even drive you know; he has to walk or take a cab."

"I know that. You think Peter can't handle that? He's been with me almost twenty years. He can handle anything I know of. You should think twice if you think poorly of Peter. I don't know that I can call anyone a friend who thinks poorly of Peter."

"Of course I don't think poorly of him! I think he's wonderful and he saved my life! I told you, he agreed not to visit."

"He's a proud man."

"Well, me too," she said lifting her chin.

He tipped back his head and laughter bubbled from his throat, filling the room. When he looked at her again, still laughing, tears were steaming from his good eye down his brown cheek. "Well, maybe you are, little girl. Maybe you are."

He got up to go, then turned back and put a hand on her shoulder.

"Is it working?" he asked, nodding to the pouch.

"Yes," she whispered. "Thank you."

He gave her his lopsided grin. "You get well," he said. "You got friends waiting for your return. Human and equine!"

IA Moore

When Billie was gone, she picked up the pouch and closed her eyes. *Friends waiting,* she thought. *Peter's waiting.*

Soon she was safe, back in her meadow of blue flowers and circling horses.

CHAPTER 13

"Hi," Abby said as she barged through the door, startling Shadow who'd been watching the tree leaves waving in the breeze.

"Oh, it's you Abby," was all Shadow could manage.

"Hey, what's with you? You look like you're in outer space."

"Sorry. You surprised me." Shadow tried to give her visitor a cheery smile, then turned back toward the open window. Feeling the warm breeze, she made a wish that when she turned around again, Peter would be sitting at her bedside in Abby's place. She hadn't seen him in so long! She longed for him to come and take her from the hospital and outside to the river.

Finally, she turned back, and found that her wish hadn't worked. "How's it going?" she asked Abby.

"Boy, did I have a lousy day!" the woman exclaimed. "Horse reared and dumped me on the way to the track. Ripped the reins right out of my hands and ran home, wrapping herself 'round a garbage truck on the way. Trainer bawled me out madder 'n hell and I couldn't get in a damn word. He's the one who should've sent a pony with the goofy mare. No use in telling him that, though, 'cause he knows, just won't admit it. Then Paul's late meeting me for lunch and Georgia's on my back because I forgot all about driving her to her mother's. Shit!"

"You really know how to cheer a person up," Shadow said, trying not to laugh.

"Wha ... oh, yeah, thanks. Glad you're not me, huh?" Abby popped her bubblegum.

"Something like that," Shadow agreed.

There was a pause. "I'm really sorry for what happened to you. Crowe was never a nice guy, but I didn't think he was capable of doing what he did."

She took a deep breath, about to answer, but Abby cut her off.

"And I heard about the bun in the oven. Don't you feel bad about that. My mom had four kids, and no husband till the third. I remember, 'cause I was the first, so don't think you're the only broad ever got herself in trouble."

Shadow clenched her jaw. She had no intention of discussing her pregnancy with Abby. "Did you ever think of having children, Abby?" she asked, changing the subject to Abby instead of herself.

"Too much work, too much dull boring work," Abby began, then stopped as if reconsidering her words. "I mean for a chick like me who likes the fast lane; for you, well, you look like the kind of girl who was born with a cute little baby all wrapped up in a pink blanket in her arms."

Shadow laughed. "You think?"

Racing Shadows

Abby tilted her head and stared, as if examining Shadow. "Yes, you do. Honest. You're just the type. Me, I never even played with dolls."

"I didn't either," Shadow admitted.

"Well, we've got something in common, then. Maybe I could be like a godmother?"

Before Shadow could reply, Abby moved to the window. "Damn hot in here. Want this window closed?" Not waiting for an answer, she cranked the little handle that closed the window.

"So what ya gonna do? Keep the kid or what?"

"I'm keeping my baby," Shadow said, surprised at how confident she sounded as she said it.

Abby smiled broadly. "Hey. I thought you would. Takes guts, you know."

"Yeah, sure," Shadow said.

"I know how you feel," Abby sympathized. "Can't follow the track with a kid in tow. Just don't work. Know some girls who tried. For the guys, it's different. They can leave the kids at home base with their wives. It's not so easy for us."

Shadow watched her as she said this, noting the change in her tone, the hint of regret. And she surmised that all her tough talk about fast lanes wasn't the whole story. Likely, the decision not to have children hadn't been easy for her. Kids or horses? Which would it be? For her, the horses won. "Yeah. I'd already thought of that," Shadow said.

"Yeah, well. I guess you gotta decide for yourself. Right?"

"Right."

"You know you got a job at the track if you want one."

"I know." Shadow realized if she kept the baby, she couldn't keep working at the track. Not many sitters were willing to start work at four in the morning and sometimes until nine or ten at night. She'd have to find something with normal hours.

Abby shook her head. "You've got a tough row to hoe, girl."

"Tell me about it," Shadow replied. "But it's getting late. I'm sure you have things to do and places to go. Fast lane and all."

Abby chuckled. "I do have a way of tiring people out. If you wanted me to shut my cake hole, you could've said so."

Shadow grinned. "Not at all! I'm really glad for the visit. Unfortunately, they give me a lot of drugs that make me feel tired—stuff for pain and who knows what else."

Abby reached into the pocket of her jeans. "Here's a letter, by the way. From Peter, little fella works for Billie."

Shadow reached out to take the letter, then set it on her blanket.

"Well, aren't you gunna open it?" Abby asked.

"Maybe a little later. After I've had a rest."

"Uh huhhh," she said, winking.

Shadow frowned.

"I think the guy's sweet on you."

Racing Shadows

"Where do you get those expressions you use?" Shadow asked her, grimacing.

"Grew up with 'em. Why change a perfect saying, eh?"

"Yeah, why?" Shadow echoed.

"Read it," Abby commanded.

"Go to hell!"

Abby began to laugh so loud that Shadow shushed her. Shadow could feel her cheeks heating with embarrassment.

"Come on, what does Peter have to say?" Abby made a grab for the square white envelope, but Shadow snatched it out of her reach, then tucked it behind her back.

"You're not having it!" Shadow said firmly.

"Well, maybe then I just better leave, give you some time alone to recuperate." She had a big smile on her red lips. Shadow was starting to get angry, thinking of something cutting to say to the woman, just when she reached out for Shadow's hand and squeezed it. "I'm just teasing you, honey. And I brought you something. For the baby."

Shadow felt her face redden even more.

"I didn't have a chance to wrap it." From out of her bag, she pulled an oval piece of red and black cloth about two feet long and a foot wide, knit in whorls like a braided rug. She spread it out in front of her, on Shadow's lap.

Shadow's mind searched through the items that babies needed. What could it be? Not a blanket, not a piece of clothing. Something to change diapers on? "It's very pretty," she said, which it was, but…

"It's a pommel pad from the Widener Stable. Old groom name of Coleman gave it to me when I was fifteen. Must be a hundred years old. See the initials?" She pointed to an embroidered G.E.W. in one corner. "They did things right in those days. Give it to your kid for her first pony. It's good luck; it's a piece of history."

"I … don't know how to thank you," Shadow mumbled.

"It's nothin'. I'm always givin' stuff away. Everybody here is always givin' stuff away. You'll find that out. See ya 'round."

Shadow watched her walk out the door with a typical jockey swagger, but she did it better than the guys.

When Shadow was sure Abby was gone and wouldn't pop back in, she slipped her hand behind her back. The envelope felt warm and soft. She laid it on the pommel pad, which she now recognized for what it was; remembered seeing them on some horses in the past.

She sat motionless for several minutes, the envelope in front of her. She wanted to open it but was afraid. Why was he writing her? Did he want to tell her something he'd find too hard to say to her face? Like he was marrying the woman he told her about, or like he didn't ever want to see her again, or like he was going down to the US … have a good life, goodbye?

Racing Shadows

David often told her, "Refusing to acknowledge a thing doesn't alter the reality of its existence."

Sighing, she forced her thumb beneath the flap and tore the envelope open, ignoring the sting of a paper cut. Inside was one piece of paper, folded twice. She lifted it to her lips—smooth. As she unfolded the sheet, she told herself that she could handle whatever it said.

She began to read.

Dear Shadow,

I didn't answer your question that day—about if I could ever love you. Quite frankly, you are so beautiful and kind that I'm afraid you're too good to be true—too good to last. I'm afraid that one day, you'll just disappear.

What I'm trying to tell you in this letter is that I care about you very deeply, and if I can get up the courage, I will love you as much as any man could.

But please don't rush into things, Shadow.

I can sense that you're not ready, even if you tell yourself that you are. And most of all, over everything else, it's important that we remain friends.

It's often seemed to me that you totally forget that I'm a dwarf. I know that most trackers don't seem to notice. But on another level, I'm sure they realize. I'm sure they take it into consideration. Do you?

Please hurry and get well.

Your friend—or more—for as long as you want me to be.

Peter

IA Moore

Shadow's heart raced fast as a runaway horse. She could barely believe what she'd read, so she read it again: all the tiny, perfect, black letters, the perfect words they formed. He said that he cared about her—he said he was her friend. She thought her heart might explode.

CHAPTER 14

The next day, Shadow showed Peter's letter to David.

"What do you think?" she asked when he looked up from reading it.

"He sounds sincere to me. The important thing is, *What do you think?*"

She shrugged. "At first, I was ... I felt really excited and happy to get this letter. I like Peter a lot. Actually, I think I love him. He's so easy-going and sweet. And I find him very attractive."

David raised his eyebrows at this—a miniscule amount maybe, but she caught it.

"He is. Really. You should see him!" Shadow insisted. "He looks exactly like Peter Dinklage. When I first met him, I *thought he was* Peter Dinklage!"

"Go on," he said.

"But..." she paused.

"But you're unsure of something?" he prompted.

She nodded, chewing at her fingernail, then clasped her hands together before replying. "Well, I think I can trust him. One time, when we were alone in a horse's stall, I told him to make love to me. I'm ashamed now—but I know I wanted to strike out at him if he tried. But he didn't: he refused."

"You believe that your trust of him is based on this incident? Perhaps you now perceive him as being asexual?"

She nodded. "Maybe a little." How did he seem to know everything?

"While at the same time, realizing full well that he's not?" he continued.

"Yes."

"You know," he said, "a dwarf is, outwardly, asexual to many people. But on the other hand, a dwarf can also be a strong sexual symbol—a little man or … a large penis."

She grimaced.

"Did you ever fantasize lovemaking with Peter?" he asked.

"No," she said. "Not really. Just cuddling and kissing."

"Do you think you're afraid of sexual intercourse?"

"Well, I was repeatedly and violently raped, so…"

"But you feel physically attracted to Peter," he stated.

"Yes. But it has to progress from just attraction, doesn't it?" she said with a frown. "I mean, Peter's a man. He'll eventually want … sex." She shrugged her shoulders.

"He's never rushed you in that direction, has he?"

"No."

"In fact, in his letter he asks YOU not to rush."

Racing Shadows

"Ye ... yes..." she half-stammered.

"Maybe he's as unsure about sex as you are."

She began to shake her head, then instead, tilted it in thought. She doubted that, but maybe...

David cleared his throat. "Shadow. I can't tell you that you'll ever be able to fully enjoy your sexuality. I'm not sure how many of us really can. I know for a fact that whoever makes love to you now will have to be very patient and kind. I only wish that I could..." He paused.

She looked at him sharply, her heart beginning to pound.

"...predict the future," he finished.

She blushed, embarrassed at what she'd thought he'd been about to say.

He leaned forward in the chair. "What did you think I was going to say?"

She shook her head.

"I left that statement open-ended briefly just to illustrate a point. You immediately thought I was hinting at physical intimacy between us, didn't you?"

She nodded.

"How did you feel about that? Tell me."

"I felt afraid, angry, threatened, betrayed, mad at you, and hurt."

"You fear being abused again, don't you?"

"Yes," she admitted, ashamed.

"Well, in my position as your counselor, it would be abuse, as it was in the case of Tony because he was your nominal father, it started when you were a child, *and* he was physically and sexually violent. But in an ideal male/female relationship, sex is an expression of caring and love. It's nothing to be afraid of and it's mutually enjoyable."

"I guess I know that. But it's just hard to believe it can be like that for me."

"I think you showed me the letter because you wanted advice. I can't tell you what to do. I can tell you that if, in the future, you have trouble with the sexual side of any relationship, you and I can talk it out, work on it. We could start working on it now, but, who knows, maybe it won't even be necessary." He smiled.

She smiled back. Maybe he was right.

"But what about the end of Peter's letter? Where he says that you don't act as though you realize he's a dwarf."

She shrugged.

"Shadow, can you truly love such a little man?"

"Yes," she said. "He's Peter."

He stared at her for several seconds, then slowly smiled. "You know, I believe that you can."

She took a deep breath and smiled.

"Do you want to go back now?" David asked her.

"Yes," she said.

"Are you ready?"

"Yes."

"Close your eyes. Go back to your meadow. You're safe there. Nothing can hurt you. When you're in the meadow, you will feel so rested, the grasses waving all around you, the horses shuffling, nudging, stepping

Racing Shadows

nearby you, keeping you safe from harm in the meadow. Once you're truly relaxed, you'll go back to Edmonton, back to the day before you left that city to come here. When you've re-lived the incident that led you to leave, I want you to float back to your meadow. You'll feel safe, back in your meadow. When I touch your cheek, you'll return to the present and know you're safe.

Shadow re-lived her attempt to reveal her pregnancy and suspicions to Barbara, followed by the car ride with Tony, her escape from the vehicle, and his pursuit of her through the woods.

David touched her cheek and she knew she was safe. Despite how gentle David was, she was still shaken when she awoke. In fact she felt more shaken than the first time she'd experienced that memory. She broke down into sobs. "How could I? How could I?" she cried.

After a very long time, David spoke. "I'm sorry about what happened. But how could you what?"

"How could I have let him rape me and get me pregnant?" She shook her head.

"Do you believe in God?" he asked her.

"No," she shook her head. "I mean, yes. I don't know!"

"Can you tell me why you're so upset?"

"Just ... just everything." For the first time, she completely and thoroughly regretted going back to re-live her past.

As if he had read her mind, David said, "It happened—whether you ever remembered it or not. You have to live in the real world, Shadow. You tried the other way and it didn't work. Did it?"

She shook her head, tears still splashing down. She moaned. "I feel so dirty ... and ... and guilty!"

David put has hands on either side of her face. "I know you feel that way, Shadow. But you have *nothing* to feel guilty about. None of it was your fault. And if there is a God and if the things that have been written about him are true, then He forgives you too."

She gulped air and tears and shame. "I don't want to be forgiven I don't deserve, I—"

What he said next hit her like an electric shock.

"The way that you have to forgive Tony."

CHAPTER 15

Walking through the dark to her first day back at work, Shadow felt a hundred years old. Every dozen steps or so, she stopped to rest. Walking made her breathe hard and breathing hard hurt her chest. But she couldn't stay home any longer—only three days were left before the last racing day of the season. Ahead of her, she'd seen two of the huge transport vans pulling cautiously out of the track and onto the narrow street. The stables without horses running in the next three days were already shipping. To another track in Canada or to the States.

When she arrived at the barn, she saw Peter. A tumble of feelings rushed through her mind and her heart, and she felt overwhelmed! Well, what had she expected, the first time seeing or hearing from him since Abby brought her his letter?

"Slow down," she whispered to herself. "Take it easy." As though she were talking to a half-crazed horse.

She breathed in deeply—the air was fresh, carrying the scent of summer's end.

She had managed to learn quite a bit about herself during her stay in the hospital. And one of the things she learned was that the goal of her life couldn't simply be … to be loved by a man. But that it was okay to want that too—it was natural. It was nothing to fear.

The fact that she had never had a father who loved her, that she'd been emotionally, physically, and sexually dominated by the father figure she'd trusted and loved, left her very vulnerable. And, counter-intuitively, craving male approval.

She knew that she and Peter would have to take things slowly—but she also knew she'd never rest until she found out if things could work out between them—one way or the other. She could live with either way, but she was anxious to know. To have it settled.

She took a deep breath just as Peter looked up and spotted her. He raised a hand in greeting. She wandered slowly toward his stalls. He didn't go back to work, but instead, watched her approach "Lookin' good," he told her.

Slow! She told herself and smiled. "When are we shipping?" she asked.

"Sunday. We're running two on the last day."

"Oh," she said. "Any today?"

"One in the fifth."

"Got a walker then?" she asked.

"As a matter of fact, I have." He grinned. "Copper Light. But she's the only one. After that, Billie's got another job for you."

"What?"

Racing Shadows

"Filling out some forms. Accounts, training schedules, and race applications."

"Forms!" She groaned. "What about the pony?"

"The groom that took Crowe's place is taking care of him. Name's Ringo. He's in the kitchen now. Have you eaten?"

"Have you heard anything more about Crowe?

He shook his head. "No change. Ruled off the track, in prison, awaiting his trial." He shrugged. "You eaten?" he asked again.

She shook her head. "I don't feel very hungry though."

He looked her up and down. "You must've gained twenty pounds since I last saw you."

Instinctively, her hand moved to her belly. "Did not," she snapped. Then she smiled and admitted, "Only fifteen."

"I would hope you'd gained—last time I saw you at the hospital, you were skin and bones."

"Paul's mom fattened me up quickly when I was allowed home," she explained.

He smiled, put a halter and shank on the little red filly, and quickly brushed her off. "Here," he said, and Shadow took her away, down the shed row. She was glad the filly was so quiet and easy to walk. She even stopped without pulling at each end of the barn and waited while Shadow caught her breath. She watched Peter's progress on the stall as she passed, but once he'd finished it, he disappeared.

In a few minutes, he returned and told her to put Copper away. The filly was warm, but hadn't sweated up at all. *A nice sensible horse,* Shadow thought as she turned to walk out of the stall. When she stopped to duck under the stall webbing, she found Copper had followed her, laying her head on her shoulder from behind. She turned and kissed her soft nose.

"Here," Peter said once Shadow was out of the stall. "Take this into my room and eat it. That's an order. Whenever Billie's not here, I'm in charge." He handed her a small cardboard box that felt warm to the touch and a tin of orange juice.

She sighed and stared at him for a few seconds. "Okay," she finally said "But you didn't have to. I could've gone myself."

"I wanted to."

She turned away so that he couldn't see her smile. "I'm in number five," she heard him call from behind her.

She opened the room door and switched on the light. Aside from the fact that it was small and that the light was a bare bulb, it looked like a real room. She ate at a small kitchen table pushed up against the window. When she'd finished, she got up to leave, then hesitated, looking back at the single bed covered with a bright red-and-blue checked blanket. *Peter sleeps here.*

Hesitantly, she approached the bed, then sat down, trying to get the sense of him here, trying to imagine how it would feel to be lying here next to him. But, she couldn't.

Racing Shadows

Instead, she leaned back against the white concrete wall, picking up the magazine that was on his night stand. *The Racing Horse.* July, 1960. On the front cover was the chestnut filly, Constantine, under Bernard Adler, winning the New York Filly Triple. She opened the magazine in her lap and flipped through the pages.

Some of the photos were of horses at stud: Northland, Vintage Nobility, Artistic Sands, Strange Moonlight… Which would she choose if she had a mare? She read the names, ran her eyes across the lines of their backs, legs, necks, stared into their unmoving, shaded eyes.

A soft quick knock and the door opened.

"Just looking at your magazine," she said, holding it up, embarrassed to be sitting on his bed.

"Go ahead," he said. "Have a nap, if you like. Billie won't be in for another hour. I'll lock the door behind me and no one will bother you."

She did feel tired. She put the magazine back on the night table as soon as he left, pulled off her boots, set them neatly beside the bed, and lay down on top of the covers, her head on his pillow. She then quickly fell asleep.

At the clang of something metallic hitting the sidewalk outside the room, she woke up, bolting to a sitting position. She'd dreamt that Peter was in the room with her, very slowly taking off her clothes. When she was totally naked, he asked her where she wanted to go and she replied, "To the meadow." He began to pick her up in his arms just as she woke up.

Rubbing her hands roughly up and down her legs, she tried to erase the sensuous feelings of the dream—she didn't want traces of them to show. Then she checked her watch: eight o'clock.

When she stepped out of the room, she saw Billie walking beside some of his horses on the road to the track. "You could have woken me up!" she shouted over to Peter, who was washing a horse. He waved her comment away. When she reached him and the horse, she took the shank from the exercise boy, who nodded his thanks and trotted off to his next mount. "I'm not totally useless, you know," she told Peter.

"I know. Billie's got the books for you to do."

She made a face at him. "Do you think Billie will take me to Birchthorn?" she blurted.

He was washing the horse's belly, barely having to bend over to do it. She noted that if he were kicked, he'd catch it bad, in the chest, neck, or face. She kept the horse distracted.

"Nope," he said without looking at her.

"Shit!" she said loudly as the horse swung around, almost knocking Peter down.

"Hey! Smarten up!" he shouted.

Shadow shanked the horse and stood him back on the rubber mat.

"Sorry," she said, embarrassed that she'd made a mistake, hurt that he'd so bluntly put her in her place.

Racing Shadows

Maybe she didn't belong here after all, maybe she didn't belong anywhere, maybe...

"Not your fault," he said.

"But you yelled at me."

"I was talking to the horse, Shadow," he replied, grinning.

She took a deep relieved breath. When she asked if she could walk the horse, she was surprised when Peter said yes. And proud ... until ten minutes later, when she was so shaky, she wished she hadn't made such a dumb request. When she finally put the horse away, she was too weak to lift a full bucket of water and carry it to the stall. From behind her, Peter reached out and took it. "Billie wants you in the office now," he said.

Shadow dragged herself round the corner and into the barn's office. "Here I am," she told Billie, who was reading something.

"Suzy, just the person I wanted to see."

She didn't bother correcting him.

He showed her what he wanted done and how to do it, telling her where to find the empty office she could use.

Shadow thanked him and started out across the grass to the racing offices that were located in the same brick building as the kitchen. She looked down at the ground as she walked. When she noticed her belly, she actually smiled.

David had asked her how she felt about having Tony's baby, the possibility of feeding it from her breast and holding it in her arms. Could she stop herself from associating it with Tony? Would she see in it the continuation of the bloodline of a man who had found it not only acceptable, but also enjoyable to abuse, rape, and torture her? He told her to seriously think about that.

Pain had ripped through Shadow when he said that—she was hurt that he would think she could feel that way about her child ... or any child.

But she did as he asked and thought it through. The result was that she couldn't detect that feeling in herself at all. A baby was a baby. If mothers were capable of feeling that way, every abused wife would hate her children, wouldn't she? A child wasn't its father, it wasn't its mother, it was itself.

The only fear she had was that of her baby turning out to be a girl. A girl like herself.

She didn't want any child of hers to ever feel the same way she had felt: weak ... dirty ... helpless. David had told her that some incest victims feared giving birth to a boy—afraid that they'll physically abuse a defenseless male, after what had been done to them by their own fathers.

Shadow could understand their fear. But knew she did not have it herself.

As she walked through the main doors and viewed the row of offices, she cursed under her breath as she realized that she'd forgotten which one Billie had told her it was. She stood like a fool in the hall, trying to remember. She heard the screen door open behind her

Racing Shadows

and moved aside to let whoever came in pass by, surprised to see it was Peter. "What are you doing here?" she asked.

"I'm running a horse today," he replied.

She looked at him, puzzled.

"I bought Copper. She's mine."

Her surprise must have shown on her face because he laughed.

"You coming with me to watch her run today?" he asked.

She nodded. "Sure." Then she asked him if he knew where she was supposed to work.

Peter led her to a vacant office and showed her a desk that held a computer and a cardboard file box with Billie's name on it. He took a seat in the chair across from it. She looked at him, expecting him to say something, but he didn't. He just sat, seemingly studying her.

"Well, I guess I'd better get to work," she said. He didn't leave, just sat and watched her. She felt herself start to blush and looked down.

"Do you want to sit in the owner's box with me, sit in the stands, or go down to the rail?" he asked her.

"Whichever you'd prefer."

"After the race, once she's cooled off and put away, will you come to supper with me?"

She smiled. "Sure."

"Thank you." He let out a sigh. "I was afraid you'd say 'no.'" A broad smile lit up his bearded face.

She narrowed her eyes, trying to figure it … him … out. Could he really have been afraid she'd say no? As he walked out of the room, she asked, "Is she going to win?"

He turned and pointed at her. "Three o'clock. In the paddock. You tell me!"

She laughed. "You're on."

The paddock looked beautiful: dark-leafed shade trees dotted the inner grass circle, which was crayon green against the red shale of the walking ring. The bright white paddock fence was lined with huge red, pink, and yellow flowers. It felt so different to be standing inside the paddock watching other people working. Now she was one of the decorations!

Abby had driven Shadow to town for lunch when she'd finished her paperwork. When Shadow told her she was going to be in the paddock with Billie and Peter, she insisted that Shadow needed a dress. Despite her protests, Abby swore that nothing less would do.

"You have an image to keep up—it's the Sport of Kings after all," she said theatrically.

So shopping they went, Abby finding her an outfit at a clothing store: a white cotton cable-knit tunic and skirt, the skirt buttoning up the back and the tunic cut in a way that bared one shoulder. The honeyed tones of her own skin against the snow-white fabric shocked her at first, but Abby wolf-whistled when she came out of the change room in the outfit, insisting it was perfect

Racing Shadows

and found her shoes, a wide brimmed white hat, and pearl drop earrings.

"You'll knock 'em dead," Abby said. "Can barely even tell you're pregnant."

If Abby hadn't come and visited Shadow so often at the hospital and grew to become a friend, Shadow might have been annoyed with the comment, but lately nothing Abby said bothered her.

The horses weren't in the paddock yet, only Billie and Shadow and some grounds people. Billie was looking over a racing program while Shadow shaded her eyes and looked toward the barns. The horses would be coming soon. Peter would be walking beside Copper Light, making sure everything was all right. Ringo would be leading her. Finally, Shadow caught sight of a black-faced horse coming through the "tunnel," which was a narrow path enclosed by chain-link fence leading to the paddock. Security staff kept spectators a safe distance from the horses.

She touched Billie's arm. "They're coming," she said, excited.

He chuckled. "Calm down."

"Sorry, I'm just so nervous," she apologized, smiling at him.

"Peter won't recognize you, you know," he said. He took her hand and tucked it into the crook of his arm. "You're a knockout today."

"Don't be silly," she said. "I just put on a dress is all. You want me to look good standing beside you in front of all these people, right?"

"Sure do," he agreed as he straightened his tie. "Look!" He pointed, stabbing the air with his finger. "Here they are. The big owner and his big horse."

Copper Light had just stepped into the ring, her red-gold coat shining like a silk stocking under the sun. Ringo was on her near side, Peter on her far. Peter stopped, letting Copper and Ringo walk on ahead. Then he crossed in front of the next horse, a grey, and jogged over to Shadow and Billie.

Shadow's hand was still tucked in the crook of Billie's arm. Peter smiled at her. She was afraid that he would say something funny and, if he did, Shadow was fully prepared to kill Abby.

Instead, he merely nodded, tilting his head back slightly to look up at her. Their eyes locked for several seconds until she started to blush and looked away.

Billie excused himself and walked over to another trainer who had just come into the paddock, leaving Peter and Shadow standing where they were, watching the filly walk the ring.

"Who's up?" she asked.

"Jessie."

"What do you expect the filly to do?" she asked him. "Really?"

"She's well-bred, but she needs to mature. This will be her first and last race for me this year."

"It will?"

"I'll take her out of training over the fall, winter, and spring, then try again next summer."

Racing Shadows

Shadow was surprised. "Can you wait that long?" she asked. "The money...."

He shrugged and smiled. "Call me unorthodox."

"But the money!"

"If she wins this, and I say IF, she'll have more or less paid for her break already."

"Has she got a shot?"

"Look at her," he replied.

Shadow studied the filly. She'd grown more solid and a little taller than when Shadow had first seen her. And she wasn't as quiet here as she was at the barn. She had a nice spring in her step. Her legs were clean and unblemished. Her chest was deep in front, whipping back up to her trim waist. She looked good. Shadow narrowed her eyes at the competition. Nothing impressive except a big-boned, rangy bay wearing the number eight. The filly had massive shoulders, a large head for a thoroughbred, and solid hindquarters. Silently, Shadow reached for and took Peter's race program. Number eight. Florence Moose. Bay filly, three. The race would be between her and Copper. The smallest horse, Copper, against the biggest, Moose.

Peter must've read her mind. "Moose is the one to beat."

She nodded. "Copper's such a sweet thing that I feel sorry for her going up against that monster!"

"Don't worry. She's tough. Like you."

"Is that why you don't worry about me?" She grinned at him.

"All right," he admitted. "I'm a little worried. But, she can do it. If it's her day, I know she can do it."

"And she's sharp today—it looks like this could very well be her day," Shadow said. Again, she watched her. Her coat shimmered, the muscles dancing beneath it. She wasn't nervous, just feeling good. She seemed to know today would be special. Just watching her move filled Shadow with awe.

"Looking more than a little keen, isn't she," he agreed.

"Why did you buy her?" Shadow asked him.

He shrugged. "Her owner wanted to send her to the States to run her through the fall and winter, hoping to win as many races as he could as soon as he could. He's the impatient type. Billie told him that Copper should take the winter off and not run again until at least next spring. Owner didn't agree and was going to take her to another trainer, so ... I made him an offer he couldn't refuse."

"Do you own any other horses?" she asked.

"None racing right now. But I have a broodmare at Billie's farm, and a yearling from her by Northern Vodka."

"Northern Vodka? Nice."

He nodded.

Silently, Shadow watched the horses filing into the shed for saddling. Not able to stop herself she asked, "Why the hell are you working as a groom if you have that kind of money?"

Racing Shadows

"You know horse racing: on top of the charts one day, up to your armpits in debt the next."

She gave him a look. She estimated Northern Vodka's stud fee to be at least ten grand. Probably more. "Why take such a risk then?" she asked him.

He shrugged. "Because I enjoy it."

Shading her eyes, she smiled into the sun as he left her in the paddock, on his way to the shed to saddle his filly.

Once the riders were up and the horses headed out onto the track for the post parade, Peter and Shadow followed behind them, pausing at the gates. "Which way?" he asked. "I'm fine with either." Considering briefly, she chose the grandstand over the owner's box or rail.

"Good," he said. "I know the best place. Where we can get an ice cream and sit alone—with a great view of the quarter pole."

They walked across the pavement, past lawns and flower beds, then up a stairway to the dim interior of the building. "Just a minute," Shadow said. "I'm betting."

"On who?"

"The best horse in the race, of course."

She smiled as she took the ten-dollar win ticket on Number Three, held it in her palm, felt the rightness of the bet.

She turned to see him waiting. He guided her to a kiosk. "Hot dog? Ice cream? Popcorn?"

"Ice cream," she replied.

"Two vanilla cones," he ordered.

Outside again, they climbed up more stairs, until arriving at rows of shining red seats, high above everything and everyone. She picked a seat at the far end of the top row. "This is fantastic," she said as they sat. "You can see everything from up here!" The view of the track, with its infield lakes, flowers, and velvet green turf was magnificent.

"Look." He reached across her to point. "There's our barn."

"It's like we're on top of the world."

"We're on top of *our* world," he emphasized.

She looked around. "And all alone."

"Can I help it if nobody else has taste?"

She smiled, her heart full, feeling as though she didn't ever want to come down as they sat side-by-side eating the sweet white ice cream.

A deep voice began announcing the horses, owners, trainers, and jockeys. When he came to Copper Light, he announced, "Copper Light, a chestnut filly, three years old, ridden by Jessie Gowan, owned by Peter Markman, and trained by Billie Moon."

Shadow reached over for Peter's hand and squeezed it. "Good luck," she said.

When she tried take her hand away, he held onto it, briefly, sending a slice of something bitter-sweet through her belly.

After parading in front of the stands, the horses were now into the clubhouse turn, warming up for the

Racing Shadows

race and approaching the starting gate. It was three minutes to post time.

Shadow looked over at Peter. He was wearing a different suit, of lighter cloth, but still dark in color. She couldn't help loving the way he looked, his face, his eyes, his hands....

She smiled.

He smiled back. "So beautiful." He touched the side of her neck with the back of his fingers. "You'd make a fantastic horse. I'd buy you in a minute. Then turn you loose."

"What if I stayed?" she asked.

There was a loud crackle and then, "They're at the post. They're off!" The announcer's voice boomed across the afternoon sky as the gates clanged open, Moose charging out first, her legs churning up toward the sky instead of straight ahead, and she lost ground and was passed.

"Better Sister takes the lead on the outside, Florence Moose behind her, Never Say No is moving up on the inside, with Copper Light holding her position between horses, followed by Egyptian Dancer, Fanjet's Glut, Little Princess Kong, and trailing is Com'on Moonshine.

"Moving down the backstretch now, Better Sister is holding the lead, but Florence Moose is moving up along her on the inside. Losing ground is Never Say No. Copper Light is racing in fourth position."

Shadow clenched her hands, her eyes glued to the group of horses racing on the back loop of the track.

"Fifth is Fanjet's Glut, sixth Egyptian Dancer, followed by Little Princess Kong and trailing still is Com'on Moonshine. Moving toward the far turn, Florence Moose has taken the lead on the rail, Better Sister losing ground, Copper Light now making her move on the outside passing Never Say No, then it's Fanjet's Glut, Little Princess Kong, Com'on Moonshine, and Egyptian Dancer."

Shadow held her breath and silently begged: *Just keep her safe, please keep her safe.*

"Coming around the far turn and into the stretch Copper Light has taken the lead by a head, Florence Moose runs second, Better Sister third. No, wait!"

Shadow gasped, the wind suddenly knocked out of her.

"Florence Moose takes the lead as Copper Light falters, Better Sister and Never Say No battling for third, then Little Princess Kong, and in the stretch run it's Florence Moose followed by Copper Light fighting to make up lost ground, Never Say No holding onto third and down to the wire it's Florence Moose by half a length, Copper Light, Never Say No, Better—"

"Did you see us get pushed out on that turn?" Shadow cried. "That wasn't fair!"

Peter patiently watched the rest of the horses cross the finish line until the last, the grey Egyptian Dancer, galloped over it, then turned to her and smiled. "Don't throw away your ticket. She got bumped bad," he said.

"I know. I practically felt it."

"What?" he asked.

Racing Shadows

"Nothing. You saw it?"

"Clear as daylight. Jessie will lodge a complaint for sure."

Shadow sat back, releasing a long stream of air from her lungs. "There's a chance she's got it, then?"

"Up to the stewards, but I think so. Let's get down there." He took her arm, helping her to her feet.

As they made their way down the steep stairs, the announcer said, "Hold onto your tickets, folks. The inquiry sign has gone up. The rider of number three, Copper Light, has lodged a claim of foul against the unofficial winner, Florence Moose, number eight." Peter took her hand, quickly squeezing it. "Cross your fingers."

By the time they made it out to the winner's circle, the result was final: the claim of foul had been allowed and Copper Light was the official winner of the fifth race.

The sweat-darkened horses, both of whom had been walking in tight circles outside the winner's enclosure, split: Florence Moose heading back to her barn, Copper Light strutting into the Winner's Circle. Peter handed Shadow the filly's lead for the picture and whispered, "You're my good luck charm." Shadow touched her lips to the filly's pink nose, silently congratulating her on her win and the horse grabbed her hat between her teeth and pulled it off. Shadow tossed her head, her hair flying in the breeze, tangling with Copper's mane as the photographer snapped the win photo.

Shadow felt so close to everyone on the track: the horses, Peter, Jessie, Billie, Abby, and Paul. In the time she'd spent recuperating at the house, she even got to know Georgia. Things were different at the track— everyone seemed to accept her, to perhaps even understand her. Or was it she who'd changed?

Reluctantly, Shadow handed Copper back to Ringo, who took her away. She turned back to Peter, who was smiling as wide as if he'd won Olympic gold. That was probably just about how he felt—his new horse breaking her maiden against horses more highly rated. Side by side, Shadow and Peter started back through the building to cash her ticket, but then she decided not to. She decided to keep it and place it in the corner of Copper's win photo, which she'd buy and frame. That way, the good luck would never change, for either her or Copper.

When Copper returned from the test barn and was bathed, cooled out, and bedded down in her stall, Peter returned to his room where Shadow had been waiting for him, relaxing on his bed.

"Ready?" Peter asked. "Ringo will feed and water off for me."

She looked at her watch. *Four-thirty.* "Isn't it early?"

"Not if we want to spend some time at the river."

She smiled and nodded. "Ready." In actuality, she could barely hold in her excitement.

CHAPTER 16

A cab drove them to the river, where Peter had the driver turn into what appeared to be an historical site—a huge, curving concrete structure with pillars. Shadow knew there'd be a plate with an inscription someplace, telling them what it was and why it was here. She forbade Peter to find it and read it because she hated history and it was probably about fighting Indians or something.

"Don't you want to know what happened here? What happened in the past?" he asked.

"I'm having enough trouble with the present," she told him, looking the other way. She'd dealt with her past at the hospital, and finally, her flashbacks were gone and her past made sense. According to David, however, there was at least one thing left to do—forgive Tony. But that wasn't something she was ready to tackle.

"Well, can I at least get a drink?" he asked.

She turned around. "Where?"

He pointed to a fountain.

She hesitated. "It looks okay ... but don't read anything."

He shook his head, chuckling to himself. Shadow wandered away toward some gardens. Ahead of her spread a variety of small ornamental trees planted in rows, and between them, huge beds of flowers. She walked toward the flowers slowly and, when she got there, breathed in their fragrance, which was so lovely, so heady, that she wanted to lie down among the blooms and bask in their fragrance all night long. She could do without food—the scent of flowers would be plenty.

She began to sit down in the grass when Peter called to her. "Hey, don't. You'll get dirty!"

She turned. The thought hadn't occurred to her that she was wearing white, she was so used to wearing jeans.

When he reached her, he took off his jacket and laid it down on the grass. "I don't want you to spoil your dress."

"If I had any common sense, I wouldn't have bought a white one," she said, sinking down onto the jacket as he sat down beside her.

"Your skin," Peter said, "in that white dress..." He raised his hand as if to stroke her shoulder, but pulled it back.

"Smell the flowers?" she asked, to distract him from making remarks that might make her face flush and her heart skip beats.

"Yes. And the river."

"Hmmm," she said, taking in the smell of the water.

He reached over, picking her a flower.

Racing Shadows

"Oh, no!" she said, looking around. "Are you supposed to do that?"

"Don't worry. I've got enough on me for bail."

She took the beautiful red flower from his fingers. "Thank you."

"Know what it is?" he asked.

The blood-red flower was as almost as big as a saucer. She tossed her head, placing the flower into her hair. "No, what is it?"

"Beats me."

She groaned. "I thought you knew!"

"Did I say I knew?" he asked with feigned innocence.

"Let's go see the river," she said, and they got to their feet and walked through a grove of birch trees, then beneath a few willows that grew by the breakwall.

"I love coming here in a storm," he said. "Some winters, the water freezes in sheets over that wall, caught in mid-air, then stays that way till spring."

"In mid-air?"

He nodded. "Just as if, in the middle of the storm, God said, 'STOP!'"

She smiled. "You come back to Fort Eldon during the winter?"

"Just once in a while, to see my horses at the farm and visit a friend."

"Oh."

They walked until they reached the breakwall. She leaned over it into the rushing sound of the water.

"Careful," he said. "Don't fall."

"I'm not that clumsy!" she protested

"Stranger things have happened. The wall could suddenly give way with you leaning against it."

Shadow drew back a bit. "The friend you visit, does she come here with you? To the river?" she asked.

"I brought her in a cab once. But she didn't get out."

But he brought her, before he brought me. "Maybe I should just jump in," she said, suddenly saddened.

"Do you mean that, because if you do…."

"If I do, what?"

"Then I might as well too."

"Don't be stupid! Why on earth would you?"

"Well, I've got as much reason to do it as you do."

"Oh, you think so, do you? I don't notice you're pregnant!" Tears gathered behind her eyes and she could already kick herself for starting the conversation. She'd more or less recovered from the assault by Crowe, and was coming to grips with her painful past. But when she thought about the future…. About how her decision to keep her baby would make it impossible for her to follow the horses as they moved on to different race tracks. About how she'd have to be alone with … with her thoughts, with the knowledge that the baby in her arms was Tony's.

Maybe David was right. Maybe she wouldn't be able to deal with the fact that the baby's father, who was her own nominal father, raped her. She couldn't know if the infant would resemble her or Tony. Might the thought of endless days and nights of being reminded of

Racing Shadows

Tony every time she looked at her own child become unbearable? Could she truly handle that?

"Shadow, what's wrong with being pregnant?" Peter asked gently.

She groaned and spoke mechanically. "Nothing. It's great."

"Look. If you want to go back to your home, I can give you the money to do so."

She whirled on him in a fury, started to stay something, then stopped. It wasn't his fault. He didn't know about the abuse in her past—she hadn't told him a thing. "Sorry," she mumbled.

For several seconds, Peter watched her in silence. "There's more to it than that, isn't there? More to it than a simple pregnancy."

She sighed. "I want to keep my baby. But sometimes I get scared. I fear I won't be able to cope. I'll be all alone."

He looked at her. "You don't have to keep it," he offered. "There's adoption. But if you do keep it, I'll help as much as I possibly can, in any way you want me to."

"I've made a decision to keep it and I'm not going to change my mind. But I'm scared for it!" she cried. Then she took a deep shuddering breath, looking away from his eyes. "Not every man's nice," she said dully. As mundane as they must've sounded, the words were the closest she'd come to telling him about Tony.

"That's true..." he said, but he said it like a question.

"If … if the baby is a girl, she may be … in danger," Shadow whispered. "She may need someone to protect her." Then, she thought of her foster mother, sweet gentle Barbara, about how much she'd loved her and how much it still hurt that Barbara had failed to protect her. She began crying.

"Oh, Shadow," he said, putting an arm around her.

"It's okay," she said. Then she shivered and walked on ahead of him along the wall, the wind blowing against her face, through her hair. When she turned to look for him, he was back where she'd left him, watching her walk away from him.

"Hey," she called. "Come on!" After waiting until he caught up to her, she walked along the river beside him for a long while. They talked about everything under the sun, stopping now and again to watch the water or talk to fishermen, admiring their catch—catfish and carp, suckers and largemouth bass—until they reached a sand beach. The roped-in part for swimming was small, just enough for wading, playing, and keeping cool, no larger because of the river, its danger. The beach was almost deserted, only three children left, building castles in the sand.

"The beach is roped off for safety but it still seems a couple of people drown in the river almost every summer," Peter said.

Once past the beach, they arrived at the south end of the town. Stopping, they viewed the few run-down restaurants on either side of the narrow, winding street. He looked at her and she looked back at him. Without

Racing Shadows

speaking, they both began to laugh. "We could take a cab to Buffalo," he finally suggested, "or to Niagara Falls."

"Or we could be adventurous," she replied, "and go in there." She pointed to a small restaurant huddled between two larger buildings. The awnings were striped bright white and green and an oval sign proclaimed in fancy script, *The Edelweiss*.

"Hey, doesn't look bad at all," he agreed, then took her hand as they crossed the street, which struck her as sweet. They peered through the large window to see gleaming wooden floors, white tablecloths, and people eating. "Do you like Austrian food?"

"How do you know it's Austrian?" she asked.

"Just guessing from the name—or it could be Swiss or German."

"What does the name mean?" She looked back at the sign, "Edelweiss?"

"It's a flower that grows in the Alps."

"I don't think I've ever had German food, or Swiss or Austrian. I don't know if I'll like it."

He took her arm, just beneath where her sleeve ended. "Are you game to try a new experience?"

"You're on!" she said.

They stepped inside the double front doors, Peter holding the door so that she could enter first. A waitress spotted them and approached; then suddenly stopped. Shadow frowned, wondering what was wrong. She looked down at her belly—did she look that pregnant? Then she realized the girl was looking at Peter. Shadow laughed out loud. Peter nudged her and she coughed weakly, as though clearing her throat. "Table for two," he said with dignity.

As they walked to their table, she couldn't help but notice people looking up and staring. She tried to suck in her belly, so very scandalous being pregnant and being with a—she remembered what David had said about a dwarf sometimes representing … a large penis. She couldn't help but grin until the ugly frown on one woman's face turned her amusement sour.

Shadow shook her head at the attitude of the people in the restaurant. Nobody at the track ever stared at them or frowned at them. Why were these people so ignorant? She thought of pulling up her tunic and showing them her lumpy red bullet wound. She imagined the women shrieking and running out of the restaurant, their men chasing after them, throwing back angry looks at her, *the hussy* … and leaving them to dine in peace. Picturing such a ludicrous scene somehow made Shadow feel better. She almost told Peter. Would he have disapproved? She found it hard to control her overly vivid imagination sometimes.

Before she knew it, they had been expertly seated and handed their menus. Peter ordered them beer, hers non-alcoholic, as they discussed the menu.

The beer arrived quickly, served in huge mugs. Strangely, it tasted sweet. When she commented, Peter told her he'd ordered it with raw egg and sugar because he thought she might like it that way.

"I love it!" she said.

Racing Shadows

Peter then discussed the food, telling her what was in each dish.

Suddenly, there was a strange noise, then another, and another. The dozens of cuckoo clocks that lined the walls of the restaurant all announced the hour together. Brightly painted birds popped out of tiny doors in the clocks, cuckooing in such a jumbled manner that it was impossible to tell the time by the number of cuckoos. Everyone laughed.

"Shadow," Peter said, pulling her attention away from the clocks. "Have you decided?"

"Everything sounds so good," she replied, then she settled on something simple—Goulash, which Peter had explained was a stew of red meat and mushrooms cooked in a paprika-seasoned tomato broth, served with bread, noodles, and a salad. For himself he chose Vegan German cheese spaetzle. This surprised Shadow as she hadn't known he was vegan.

"I didn't know you don't eat meat," she said. "I hope it was okay that I ordered it. I can change my order...."

"No, don't do that. It's perfectly fine," he assured her and told the waitress that was all.

"I'm glad she's wearing a blouse under that dress," Shadow said as the waitress left the table with their order.

"It's called a *dirndl* and speak for yourself," he said.

"I guess I asked for that one," she muttered. Then she focused on the vase in front of her. "Yuk. What is this?"

"The beautiful *edelweiss*."
"This? You've got to be kidding."
"They look a little bit better when they're not dead and dried. But just a bit." He laughed.
"You've been to Europe?"
"Couple of times."
"Running horses?"
"Yeah. And visiting studs."
"Did you go to England?" she asked.
"Yes."
"What's it like, England?"
"Moist."
"No, seriously!"
"Really. That was my strongest impression—everything was so moist and green. The older buildings were covered in moss. When you walked down the country streets at night, you'd end up crunching dozens of these huge snails under your shoes—I can still remember the sound. It couldn't be helped."
"I'd stay in at night."
"No, you wouldn't. You'd come out with me and walk miles across fields full of horses and cows and hedgehogs on the way to the pub. You'd love it."
"And what would we do at the pub?"
"Drink beer, eat fish 'n' chips, and study the English."
"Sounds fascinating."
"It will be … or would be, I mean."
She pushed aside the dried flowers and stared at Peter across the table. She wanted to ask him again if he

Racing Shadows

could one day love her, the way he'd written in his letter. He stared back at her. She was about to ask when their meals arrived and she felt ravenous. She was surprised to find that she liked the food very much. She even sampled a forkful of Peter's dish, which he placed behind her teeth onto her tongue.

"Delicious," she said.

"I agree. Maybe we could come here once a week."

"You're leaving in a few days," she said.

"Right. But I will come back and visit. And there's next year too."

"Why are you a vegan?" she asked Peter.

"Because I don't want to eat animals," he said with a shrug.

"Have you never killed an animal then?" she asked, used to the fact that Tony had hunted every chance he got.

"No. Although I did take a very old dog to be euthanized at the vet's."

"That must've been sad," she said.

He sighed. "Dogs don't live long enough."

"No they don't," she agreed.

She suddenly felt bad, having eaten meat in front of him. She'd taken his word for it that it wouldn't bother him, but now was having second thoughts. Really, what right did she have to take part in the death of an animal when she could well survive eating other things. "I feel bad now," she said, "having eaten that meat."

He looked at her with a puzzled expression. "Don't. I told you it was fine with me—"

"I deserve to die, I really do," she said in a burst of despair. She sprang to her feet, ran between tables, bumping chairs, then burst through the front door and continued running, across the street. She ran along the river, her shoes falling off of her feet, the evening grass cool and moist against her soles as she ran and ran until she had to stop.

She leaned over the wall, gulping in the crisp air. The lights of a city twinkled across the river, reflecting onto the rushing water. It was dark, but moonlit, the gulls small white patches here and there on the breakwall and in the grass. Her lungs burned every time she took a breath and her knees quaked. She didn't know how long she spent looking into the darkness of the river. Nor could she put a label on what she was feeling. She knew only that she had to change, make herself into a better person—but how?

"That was a dumb thing to do, running off like that," said a voice to her left.

She sighed. "I know. I'm sorry. I just get upset really easily these days." She shook her head in dismay—she'd always been stoic.

"Hormones," he said.

"More than that."

"We missed dessert," he said. "Let's go back."

"Go back? Now?" She was astonished. How could he even think of it?

"They say that when a horse throws you, you've got to get right back on."

Racing Shadows

She smiled and turned to face him. "Is that what they say?"

"Shadow." His voice was soft. "You've got nothing to feel bad about. Honestly."

"You don't know me!" she said. "You don't know what's all happened to me. I'm not good enough!"

"Whatever happened in the past, you can do or be anything you want to now and in the future, Shadow. Whatever you think you've done so wrong in the past, you can make amends for in the way you live your life now. Deciding to keep the baby was a hard thing to do. But it was a good thing too. You can do or be anything you want," he repeated.

She stared at him in amazement. Did he actually believe that?

"But I have so much to make up for."

"I think you've suffered enough," Peter said.

"But *I* don't."

"I have faith in you," he said with emphasis. "Even if you don't. Yet."

Shadow held her hand to her belly as they started to walk back. Silently, he handed her her shoes. "I used to have this nightmare when I was a little girl," she began. "I used to dream I was a monster, ugly and covered in slime. Instead of hands and feet, I had hooves like a goat or a cow."

He didn't say anything as she stooped to put on her shoes. When they arrived back at the restaurant, he reached up and touched her forehead. "And here, did you have a horn?"

She started to laugh. "No, I did not!"

They returned to their table, which he'd had the waitress keep as they left it. For dessert, he ordered a piece of Black Forest cake and she ordered Apfelstrudel. When they finished eating, he took her hand.

"Where to now?" he asked, leaning across the table.

She shrugged. "You're the expert here. What are the options?"

"We could go to see the Falls, go to a movie, a wax museum, play mini golf.... Or we could go to Emerald Beach."

"Emerald Beach sounds nice. What is it?"

"A huge amusement park. You like rides?"

A cab took them from the restaurant, driving several miles along a highway, and then turned left down a residential street. The first thing she noticed when they got out of the cab, aside from the noise, was the smell of horses. "I smell horses," she said excitedly. "Where are they?"

Peter led her to a corral where there were several saddled ponies lined up along a rail. Shadow rubbed a brown pony's forehead. It was standing asleep and didn't seem to much notice her touch.

Just as she began feeling sorry for the animal, thinking how bored it must be, how unfree, Peter gave a man, who was dressed in rawhide chaps and a black cowboy hat, some money. Then he took her hand and

Racing Shadows

began to lead her through a chute. "You said you wanted to learn to ride."

"I said I wished I *had* learned!"

"There's no time like the present."

"Don't be silly. Look at those ponies. Look at how small they are."

"Got to start someplace. Size isn't everything, you know." He grinned.

"No. I'm not going!" She crossed her arms over her chest. "Look! I'm wearing a dress."

"Just tuck it up between your legs."

"That's easy for you to say! You're not going to look stupid."

"I'm not, eh?" he asked, then walked a few steps and put his foot into the nearest stirrup, which belonged to a black pony, swung into the saddle, and smiled at her.

She began to laugh. She couldn't help it. A dwarf dressed in a suit and sitting on a cute, hairy pony was just too funny. "I take that back," she said weakly when she'd caught her breath, looking around the corral for the largest pony. It was very pretty, chestnut with a white mane and tail and white stockings. Turning to the cowboy, she asked, "I won't hurt this pony if I ride him, will I?"

"No way, miss. He's 14-3, so actually a small horse. He can carry two hundred pounds loping a fast mile."

She cleared her throat. "Well, okay." Then she tucked up her skirt, put a hand on the pony's saddle horn, and lifted her foot toward the stirrup.

"Nope," the cowboy said. "Use the other one. The other foot."

"Oh." She'd seen this done a thousand times and still couldn't remember?

Before she knew it, the cowboy's hand encircled her ankle and guided it into the stirrup. "Hop up now," he said and when she began to, he placed his other hand on her bottom, pushing her up. She slapped at his hand and he laughed, keeping it where it was.

Jerking her leg back, she tried to kick at him, but missed, then stepped both feet back down onto the ground. Hands on her hips, she stared daggers at him.

Peter rode his pony up to where they were standing, she still glaring at the cowboy, who was trying to apologize. Then she turned from him to look at Peter.

"Don't tell me. You're not ready to ride yet, right?" he asked.

She frowned and shook her head. Then, after adjusting her skirt, she leaned on the rail and watched Peter ride.

"This isn't half bad," he said as he rode past her. "Maybe I'll buy this pony. Hay's cheaper than cab fare."

Despite her mood, she smiled. "You would, wouldn't you? Ride around the streets on this little cutie." She waved her hand toward the pony.

"Look at it this way: I've got nothing to lose by looking slightly more foolish than I already do."

"You look just fine to me," she said.

Racing Shadows

On his next turn around the corral, he walked the pony over to her and halted it. Then he looked at her for a few seconds. Reaching over, he brushed his fingertips along her bared shoulder, without saying a word. Making her shiver.

He ended up buying five trips around the corral as he illustrated to her how to stop, start, turn, trot, and canter, explaining the cues he was giving the pony.

"Are you sure you don't want to try?" he asked.

"Well, maybe I should then, before I forget everything," she conceded.

This time Peter helped her onto the chestnut horse and things went smoothly. So smoothly, she wanted to keep riding all evening. She even mastered the trot and canter as Peter and the cowboy applauded! But eventually, the cowboy told them the pony ride was closing for the night.

When they left the corral, she ran ahead to the nearest food stand and bought some candy apples to take back to the ponies.

"May I?" she asked the cowboy when they arrived back at the corral.

He nodded his head, cutting the apples in pieces with a knife he pulled out of his boot.

Once finished feeding the ponies and dripping in red dye and pony slobber, they washed their hands in a drinking fountain. Then they began walking around the rest of the amusement park to check out the rides.

The first ride they tried was called the Magic Carpet. On the ride, they navigated long, black passages

IA Moore

as wild animals and monsters sprang out at them, scaring everyone on the ride, but also making them roar with laughter. Then they braved a crooked room, lily pads, air jets, and a hall of mirrors that made her look like a dwarf and Peter look ten feet tall. The ride ended with them sitting on a carpet that rose and fell, transporting them to the ground.

Next, Peter tried his luck at the games, winning Shadow a stuffed koala bear, which she carried around in her arms like a baby.

Then they rode the merry-go-round several times until she grew too dizzy to continue. They tried the Octopus, the Wild Mouse, and the Salt and Pepper Shaker. One after another, they rode the rides. Finally, they climbed aboard the first car of the Space Rocket, which was a huge, silver roller coaster, built to extend over the nearby beach and lake. It was the only ride that really frightened her, being up so high at the top, then tipping straight down, waiting for the plunge to the ground beneath. For what seemed like forever, they hung above the beach, facing downward, her heart pounding, and she suddenly wanted a way out, wanted to run, but was trapped in that seat ... then felt Peter's hand cover hers as she gripped the bar, his warm calloused hand over hers, and she felt safe.

Before going home, they returned to the river. By then, it was even darker, the only light coming from the full moon and the stars. Peter told the cab driver to come back for them in an hour.

Racing Shadows

He took her hand and led her back to the willows. He sat down on his jacket on the ground and she followed, placing her hand on his thigh.

He stroked her arm. Instinctively, she drew away.

"Somebody hurt you," he said. "A man."

She nodded.

"How?" he asked.

"I don't want you ever to know," she replied.

"Why not?"

"You'd never ... you'd never love me if you knew."

"Shadow, what happened? He left you? Claimed the baby wasn't his? What?"

She shook her head. "No. He, my foster father..." She thought back to David, all of his clinical, distancing terms—she needed one now. "He began molesting me when I was young. When I got older and began to resist, he got more and more violent, more and more out of control ... until I had to give in, let him.... I was sure he'd kill me if I didn't." She shrugged, letting out a sigh. "No one helped me."

"Shadow," Peter said as he pulled her into his arms.

She immediately felt comfortable, safe. "When you wrote me that you want to stay friends, did you mean that?" she asked him.

"Yes. And as far as I'm concerned, it doesn't ever have to go further. The truth is, you're so beautiful, the very thought of touching you, making love to you, scares me."

"You still think I'm beautiful—now? After what I just told you?"

"Nothing could change that."

Slowly, she took off her clothes, then helped him take off his. They stretched out side-by-side on the ground, facing one another. She moved her lips close to his, so close that she could feel his breath on them. "Kiss me," she whispered. Slowly, he kissed her until her lips parted and he kissed her deeper and longer until his mouth slid down to her breast. When she spread her legs, his hand slipped between them.

"You're so warm," he whispered, his lips against hers again. "Do you want me?"

"Yes," she murmured and it was the truth. As he kissed her, he rolled her onto her back and began to shift himself over her, but when his nakedness met her flesh…

"No!" she cried. "Stop!"

And he did.

She began to sob.

"Shadow, it's all right," he said. "It'll be all right."

CHAPTER 17

When she arrived at the barn the next morning, everything was in darkness. It puzzled her that Peter hadn't started yet. *Could he be at the kitchen?* She began to walk over, then realized the smell of frying bacon would not do her any good at all. She turned toward the door of his room. Could he have slept in?

She approached the door, laid her hand on it, and pressed her ear against the smooth wood. She didn't hear a sound, just the early morning shuffling of horses from the stalls to her right.

She knocked softly. No answer. She turned the knob slowly, then pushed the door open an inch, another. Finally, when it was all the way open, she saw that he was still in bed, asleep. A rush of emotion overcame her and she felt warm at the sight of him. Until it occurred to her why he probably slept in. *Sometimes, we're up the whole night, just talking,* he'd said. She felt her gut twist. Peter was with her until one in the morning, and then he went to *her* place? *Why? Because I...?* She clenched her jaw in frustration. She hated being jealous and angry but she couldn't help it.

She began to close his door when she heard, "Shadow?" and saw him lifting his head from his pillow.

"Yes. It's me," she answered. "It's time to get up."

He laid his head back down. "Come in."

After turning and checking behind her, she took a step forward and slowly shut the door, leaving the room in darkness.

"Can you come over here?" he asked.

Reaching his bed, she knelt beside it. The room smelt like new hay, timothy. "It smells like you keep horse food under your bed," she said, unable to keep her anger fueled, feeling it dissolve like sugar cubes in warm milk.

"Come closer," he said.

She leaned forward, her hand brushing something soft on the floor and she recognized the shape. Quickly, she reached over and touched his head. You're not wearing your cap!" she said.

"Did you think I wear it to bed?"

"Well, yes. You wear it a lot!" She didn't take her hand away, instead leaving her fingers in his hair. He turned his face and she felt his lips brush the skin of her arm.

She thought that it would be so fine just to slip into the warm bed beside him, that it should be so easy just to lie there in his arms. But she stayed where she was. Finally, she said, "I can't…."

Can't what? She'd wanted him to ask her, but he remained silent.

Racing Shadows

"My legs are cramped," she complained, then stood up, losing contact with him, and walked out the door, closing it quietly. There was still no one else around so she went to Copper's stall.

The filly was awake and walked over to Shadow, resting her head against Shadow's shoulder. As Shadow stroked the horse's soft coat, she thought about the next step in her recovery and decided that she was finally ready to work on that final item David told her she'd have to tackle—confronting her feelings toward Tony, her anger and hatred, processing it, and finally, forgiving him. She sighed. She was willing to try, but the task seemed impossible.

Peter walked up behind her. She heard his footsteps on the hard-packed earth, felt his hand on the small of her back. She turned toward him, happy he'd come to her. "Shadow," he whispered. "It's okay. We've got lots of time. We've got forever."

Shadow's heart did a flip and tears filled her eyes. For better or worse, she knew she was falling deeply in love with him. Although she didn't want to, she was driven to ask, and fully expected an answer she didn't want to hear. "Why did you sleep in today?"

"One of our horses got cast. The ruckus of him thrashing around woke me up. I wrangled a couple of other guys that live on the backside and we got him to his feet, but it took a while. Then I waited with the horse until the vet came and checked him over. So, it ended up a long, late night."

"Aw, poor guy," Shadow said. A rush of relief washed over her. He hadn't been with *her* after all.

Her heart now happy, she walked Copper. Then she took out Spanky, who was running in the first. Finally, she headed over to the racing office to do more paperwork. After grabbing some lunch, she dropped by the pony's barn just to say hi.

After all that, she was exhausted. She napped on Peter's bed while he continued working. She woke up cranky, hot, and tasting dust when Peter knocked at the door.

"It's me."

"Come in," she said into the pillow as she lay face-down on the bed.

"How are you?" he asked.

"Dirty. I'm hot and dirty," she moaned.

Without a word, he left the room, but soon returned.

"What?" she asked in alarm, trying to sit up in bed when she heard the sloshing of water.

"Lie down. It's okay," he said. "I've got experience."

She frowned at the sight of him, standing there with a bucket in one hand and a sponge in the other. "I'm not a …" she began. "Is that sponge even clean?"

"Of course it's clean. We wash only clean horses here. Give me your face."

"No," she squealed, but as she tried to get up, he put a hand on her shoulder.

Racing Shadows

"Easy, now," he said. "This isn't going to hurt."

"I know it's not going to hurt, but I don't want to get wet!" She managed to shove his arm with the dripping sponge away and sit up.

"All right. All right. You win. How about just the feet?"

She tilted her head, considering the idea.

"Nice warm water," he coaxed. "On those tired little tootsies."

"Oh, all right," she huffed.

"Good girl," he said as he pulled off one of her socks. He held her foot in one hand as he washed it with the other, first stroking and scrubbing it with the sponge, then squeezing the sponge and letting warm rivers of water run over her instep and toes.

"Hmmm…" she said. "Maybe I should've been a horse. I mean, this is service."

"My pleasure," he said. After he finished washing her second foot, he toweled them both dry.

She smiled and asked him, "Why did you do that?"

He shrugged. "I dunno. Maybe just because it was fun. Why'd you let me?"

She slid off the edge of the bed and onto her knees in front of him, pressing her body against the length of his, hugging him tightly. She shivered against him in delicious craving for several minutes until, reluctantly, she let him go. Still tingling, she got to her feet, asking him, as though nothing had happened, when they were leaving.

"Ten minutes," he answered, but only after he'd taken a deep breath and cleared his throat.

She smiled. "Billie here?"

"He's just outside."

She sighed. "I have a question," she said, looking at him. "Do you wash her feet too?"

He laughed, but caught her hand as she stepped out of the room. "No," he said, before letting her go.

Copper was easy to load into Billie's horse trailer. She simply stepped up into it behind Peter. Shadow slowly closed the back of the trailer behind them as Peter climbed out of the side door. Billie waited for them in the pickup while Peter did a final check to make sure everything was secured and ready to go. Shadow watched him and then climbed into the front seat beside Billie, followed by Peter. "All aboard," Billie said. "Move 'em on, Head 'em up, Rawwwhiiide!"

"Head 'em up?" she asked.

"That's cowboy talk."

"Yeah? You know all about that stuff, do you?"

"Damn tootin' I do. Just call me Cowpoke Billie."

"And when's the last time you roped a steer, Cowpoke Billie?"

"She don't even call me 'sir' no more. You hear that, Peter?"

"Sure do, sir."

"Women. Give 'em an inch and the next thing you know, they're…."

Racing Shadows

Soon, they arrived at a long driveway lined by poplars. Billie turned in carefully, looking behind him as if to make sure the trailer followed.

"Welcome to the farm," Billie said as he pulled up into a large graveled parking area. In front of them was a large barn painted deep green. "We've got twelve stalls, ten paddocks, a huge pasture, a horse exerciser, and a training track," Billie said, pointing.

"We turn the horses out in the day, and put them inside overnight, weather allowing. The stalls are in the center of the barn and there's an indoor track around them. A person can gallop horses inside the building during the winter. One of our exercise boys, Alex, stays in Fort Eldon all winter with his family. Doesn't travel to Toronto or the US. He comes to the farm and exercises them to keep the sound ones in shape. Nothing intense, just enough to remind them they're racehorses."

They got out of the truck and walked into the barn. A few heads poked out of their stalls and turned to look at them. "Those are the horses on stall rest. The others are out in the pasture or paddocks.

"How many do you have here?" she asked.

"Seven, but two are going to Toronto in a few weeks. That leaves six counting Copper." Billie turned to her. "I have a groom name of Baxter that lives here fulltime, in the house trailer we passed on our right as we drove in here. He keeps his riding horse here as well. Now, if you think you could come in on the weekends, I could give Baxter weekends off. I wouldn't expect you to stack bales or nothing." He directed his gaze at her middle. "Just feed, water, and groom, then turn 'em out for the day, and bring 'em back in at night. Baxter will have the feeding and stalls done when you come in on Saturday morning, and on Sunday the stalls can wait until he gets back."

She nodded and he gave her a grin. "This way, you can earn yourself a little pin money, and the way Peter tells it, you might be around some, anyway."

She looked at Peter and smiled. "Yep," she said. They left the barn to go back to the trailer for Copper. On their way, they ran into Baxter, the live-in groom. He was dressed in tan riding breeches, a yellow cable-knit sweater (*in this heat*) and tall black riding boots.

His accent was strongly foreign, British or Irish maybe, as he greeted Billie. "Brung me another charge, 'ave yee, sire?"

"Yup. One of Peter's."

"Oh, hullo," he said, as if he'd overlooked Peter's presence. "And hullo to you, lass," he said to Shadow.

"This is Suzy, the girl I told you about. She'll be relieving you a couple days a week this winter."

"Jolly good! I'll have a chance to see more of the countryside this year, maybe do some bird watching."

Billie rolled his eyes. "Whatever turns you on," he muttered under his breath.

Shadow thought she knew why this guy was stuck out on the farm away from the track.

"You know, I really think they ought to get a fox hunt going out here. I don't see why not. Back in—"

Racing Shadows

"Great thinking," Billie said. "Why don't you approach the mayor about it?"

"Bloody good idea!" Baxter enthused.

When they reached the trailer, Peter climbed in the side door while Billie opened up the back. With some gentle urging, Copper stepped back down out of the trailer. Baxter rushed to her head and began fussing over her.

"Baby girl, come see your new home," Shadow heard as Baxter walked Copper to her stall. Peter shrugged as they followed. Shadow estimated that Baxter was at least six foot three: He towered over the filly, looking as though he could lift her up and lay her into her stall like a baby into its crib.

"Nice filly you've got there, Peter," Baxter said as he came out of Copper's new stall, carrying her halter and shank and hanging them on the hook by the door. "I'll have to burn a name plate for her tonight." He gestured to the signs above each stall, each horse's name burnt into an oblong slab of tree trunk. He turned to Shadow. "Do you do wood burning, Suzy?"

She shook her head. "Actually, my name's Shadow, and no, I'm afraid I don't."

"Oh right, I'm sorry. Billie's a right card. He calls all the girls who work for him Suzy."

Peter touched Shadow's arm. "Right, and I've personally seen him suffer for it," Peter whispered.

"Abby?" Shadow asked.

"You got it," he replied and they both laughed. Billie had wandered down the row of stalls checking over his charges. "I heard that!" he said.

"Shadow," Baxter said, as if to change the subject, "I was just wondering if you crochet? It's so relaxing and I see you're expecting. Perhaps we might get together some nights and make a few things for the baby."

Shadow was too shocked to respond and felt herself blush, much to her annoyance. "Ummm," she said. "I never tried, but I'm up for it if you're willing to teach me."

"Why certainly!"

Billie cleared his throat. "We've got some things to talk about," he said to Baxter.

"Cuppa tea, folks?" Baxter asked. "Maybe scones? I've got plenty."

Billie slung an arm up around Baxter's shoulder, then turned back to Shadow and Peter. "We'll be about half an hour," he said to them. "Baxter and I need to have a little chat."

"That filly got hay and water in her stall?" she heard Billie ask as the two of them made their way toward the house trailer.

"Do you have to ask?" Baxter responded, his voice cracking with what could only be offended pride.

Shadow smiled at Peter, who smiled too. "Baxter's great with the horses," he said. "Trustworthy as hell when he's not sloshed."

"He drinks?"

Racing Shadows

"Only when he binges, which is about three or four times a year. Billie will probably ask you to call him every day and report back to Billie if he's missing."

"No problem," Shadow said. "Seems like a nice guy."

"A dozen or so cats 'round here think so too," Peter agreed, and she looked up at the straw bales stacked along the exterior barn walls to see several cats sprawled out on bales or crouching in the spaces between.

She felt Peter touch her arm. "Got something to show you," he said.

She smiled. "What?"

They walked to the tack-room at the end of the row of stalls. Peter opened the door and switched on the light. Inside were several saddles plus halters, bridles, shanks, bandages, coolers, blankets, brushes, and everything else you'd expect to find in a stable.

"Very neat, isn't he?" she commented as she looked over the immaculate room.

"Oh, fastidious is the word," Peter replied, and walked over to one of the western saddles. It was made of elaborately tooled light-brown leather and sat on a quilted black pad. Looped over the horn was a matching silver-studded bridle with a snaffle bit. "I picked this up for you and Copper," he said.

"For me?" she asked, puzzled.

"Well, you want to learn to ride, don't you?"

She gave him a who-are-you-trying-to-kid look, but said nothing.

"It fits Copper, and will fit you too. I thought you might want to start riding her while I'm gone. You could start by walking her around the barn. She won't take off on you."

"Are you sure?" Shadow asked him. "I was thinking I'd start with the pony."

"I'm positive. The pony would work but he follows the track and isn't here for the winter."

"I can't do it," she blurted.

"Why not?"

"I … don't know," she admitted.

"If you want to wait until I get back to try, that's fine. When I come back next spring, I want us to meet right here. I'll bring the pony and we'll go for a ride in the big field out back."

"Me on the pony and you on Copper?"

"Or vice versa. Whichever you feel comfortable with."

She smiled, looking into his eyes. She didn't have the slightest confidence that she'd be able to function as Copper's rider, but it warmed her heart that he believed she could. That he had that much faith in her. Not to mention that he was talking about a future that involved the two of them seeing one another again! In the spring—the beginning of life, the natural time for lovers.

The track won't be gone forever, she suddenly realized. He would be back. And they would have *forever*, just like he'd said.

Racing Shadows

"Okay," she replied. "In the spring. It's a date." She reached out and took his hands in hers, whispering, "Thank you."

CHAPTER 18

Three weeks after the track left town, Shadow had settled into a routine. On Mondays, she did the week's shopping. Tuesdays, she did the laundry, and Wednesdays, she cleaned the house. Thursday, she took Mrs. Shevchuk out somewhere—window shopping, to a friend's place, a restaurant, a movie, to the library, or just for a drive. Friday mornings, she met with David, her counselor, and then, in the afternoon, she explored the town and the surrounding countryside, often with Squeaks at her side. On Saturday and Sunday, she took care of the farm.

Although there were hugs and a few tears when she said good-bye to Paul, Abby, Jessie, Georgia, and Billie, Shadow didn't see Peter off on the day he left, refusing to watch him disappear into the bowels of the huge horse transport van. It was better that way—she didn't want to break down in ugly crying and embarrass the both of them. She told herself to stay strong, that they'd meet in the spring and, and by then … by then, what?

By then, her transformation would be complete.

Racing Shadows

What transformation? Daughter to mother? Hotwalker to groom? Woman to horsewoman—what? Just what did she expect? She shook her head ... just something, that was all. Something better than what she was now.

That morning, after seeing David, she checked with Baxter about any changes in the horses' routines or feed, or any scheduled appointments with the farrier, chiropractor, or vet. She also needed to know the details on which horses Alex would be over to exercise on Sunday, so she'd know which horses to leave in their stalls that morning. Then she set off on a long walk. There was something she wanted to see.

Shadow left the house and walked along the road to the track, but instead of turning in, continued straight ahead, walking all the way down to the lake.

There, she strolled along the pale sand, just at the edge of the water. For several minutes, she stood still, simply enjoying the sound of the lapping waves, the breeze through her hair, the caress of the sun on her face, and the green smell of seaweed. Then she began to walk again, viewing her surroundings. She passed several huge houses built well back from the shore. They were set behind stone walls on grassy hills. They looked battered, undoubtedly by winds and storms, some of them appearing as if no one had lived in them for a long time.

She had the crazy desire to enter one of them in particular, a gigantic one, fronted by massive curving bay windows on each of its three floors. From where she stood, she could see that the lake water had, at some time during storms, come up and torn large boulders out of the stone wall, washing away part of the hill on which the house had been built. Branches torn from the great trees surrounding the house were scattered all about, one of them appearing, from where she stood, as though it had gone through one of the bay windows on the first floor.

That's when she decided that she'd like to own that house—take care of it, sit at those windows during a storm. As she stood, her boots sinking slowly into the light sand, and dreamt of living there, a wolf-like dog galloped around one corner of the house, hesitating when it sensed her presence. After spotting her, it tore toward her at full speed, leaping off the high wall to land in a spray of sand, not faltering a single stride.

The animal stopped directly in front of her. Lowering its head, it bared its teeth and snarled. She was glad she hadn't brought Squeaks because this dog was large enough to tear him to bits. The beast continued to stand stock-still in front of her.

"Bad dog!" she attempted. "Go home!" No response, just the breeze ruffling the monster dog's grizzled hackles. Carefully, she took a step backward and the animal took one forward. She longed to turn around and search for the person she now remembered seeing further down the beach, sitting on a log near a patch of bushes, but she didn't dare turn, didn't dare take her eyes off the dog. The dog's eyes stared into hers without blinking, glassy and cold. She could feel

Racing Shadows

her heart speeding up, then racing—she didn't want to die here by the lake, and be eaten by this beast. Gathering her nerve, she moved her hand forward, palm down, and said, "Good boy, good boy." The dog lurched forward with a harsh bark, and she pulled her hand back. In his eyes, she imagined a gleam of red.

Taking a deep breath—was this her punishment for the life she had led?—she said, "If you have to kill me, do it quickly." Then she turned on her heel and walked straight into…

"He won't hurt anyone who doesn't hurt me," said a quiet voice.

For a long time, Shadow just stared at the shape wrapped in what looked like a hooded monk's robe. Then she said, "Marjorie?"

"Pleased to meet you, Shadow," the woman replied. "You can keep walking now. Darkness won't follow you."

"Wha…?" Shadow began.

A hand emerged from beneath the woman's coat sleeve, and the dog ran to her, placing its broad head directly under her small hand.

Darkness, Shadow thought.

Later that day, Shadow sat down at her desk to write the letter she'd been putting off. She sorted through the box of pens on the desk, trying them out: testing out the smoothness with which they wrote, the hue of the ink…. Finally, she chose the one she wanted to use—a black ink fountain pen—and began. After scrawling the date on a clean sheet of white paper, she wrote, "Dear," then crossed it out and put in its place, boldly and simply, "TONY." And that was as far as she got, unable to order her thoughts, unable to put onto paper words she knew he'd be reading.

She sighed. *Maybe tomorrow, I'll feel stronger*, she thought, and instead of writing the letter, she took Squeaks out for a brief walk to pick up the mail. Sorting through it as she walked back to the house, she discovered one large pink envelope and a smaller red one addressed to Mrs. Shevchuk, whose birthday was in a week, two bills, some brochures and ... a white envelope with her name above the address. Shadow Adams—printed small and neat, and Peter's return address in the corner. Her heart seemed to drop to her toes, then bounce back up into her throat.

She chained Squeaks outside to his doghouse to enjoy the late-afternoon sun. He lay down on the grass, his head cushioned on a worn-out sneaker of Paul's that seemed to have been left there for just that purpose. Then she walked slowly and calmly up the front stairs and into the house, although she really wanted to race. She handed Mrs. Shevchuk, who was at the kitchen table sipping tea, her mail.

"You know, you should start to come with us, to the mail," Shadow told her. "It's not far and it's still warm out there. You should get out in the fresh air before winter comes."

Racing Shadows

"I think I'd like that," she replied. She opened and showed Shadow her birthday cards, smiling widely, then excused herself to read the accompanying letters.

Shadow took her own letter to her room and sat cross-legged on the bed. Fingers trembling, she tore open the envelope and pulled out a single sheet of pale-blue unlined paper. Unfolding it, she read:

Dear Shadow,
I miss you and want you to know that you are always in my thoughts.
Thank you for the way you made me feel whenever we were together. You took me seriously. You made me feel like a man—in many senses—including those of chivalry and romance. If you can imagine anything as silly as a romantic dwarf, that is.
Do you still remember our date for next spring? How is Copper?
The horses are running well at Birchthorn. Everyone here is also well, except Jessie, who broke her shoulder and is spending time with her boyfriend in New York until it heals, or should I say, half-heals. You know Jessie.
If you ever need anything, or if you just feel like talking, don't hesitate to call me here at the track. You have the number.
Your Friend,
Peter

IA Moore

Upon reading it the first time, Shadow began to cry. Sniffling, she read the letter over again. And a third time. Finally, smiling broadly, she brushed her tears away. Even though he had promised to write, she hadn't been sure that he would. She hadn't been sure he'd think of her at all once he was at Birchthorn and she was so glad that he had.

His letter, the affirmation of his friendship, made her feel stronger. Strong enough? She picked up a pen and fresh sheet of white paper, prepared to find out.

She wrote:

TONY,

I am standing here, head bowed and dressed in black, at your gravesite.

I lay to rest all the cruel and hurtful things you've done to me.

I lay to rest the power you had over me.

I lay to rest my hunger for your approval and praise.

I lay to rest my long-held fantasy that you would someday, if I only pleased you well enough, turn into the father I'd always wanted.

Taking into my hands red salve, I rub it onto your dead cold body: your eyes that laughed at me, your lips that tasted me, your hands that beat me, your feet that kicked me, and your heart ... that never knew me.

Racing Shadows

Slowly, as I rub, the warmth begins to seep back into your body. Gradually you return to life. Yes, I've brought you back to life again. But that doesn't change what I've laid to rest here today, at this, your gravesite.

Do you know what the salve is, Tony? Do you know why it is red?

It is red because it's my blood. But it's also my forgiveness.

Your Toy No Longer,
Shadow

She stuffed the letter into an envelope. It wasn't quite the letter she'd discussed with David, but it felt right.

Then she composed her letter to Barbara, explaining everything, and not sparing any detail. Including the fact that she was pregnant with Tony's baby. Shadow informed her that she needed to protect the next little girl that Barbara and Tony might foster. She told Barbara that unless she informed child services in Alberta of what Tony had done to her, Shadow would report everything to the police. She told Barbara that she expected to hear back from her that Tony's actions had been reported to child services and he was in professional treatment for his problem. Also, that he'd never be allowed to foster or adopt children again. She demanded proof of the same.

Shadow wrote the words with a heavy heart. She loved Barbara and didn't want to put her through the pain she was sure her letter would cause, but at the same time, knew that it had to be done. After signing Barbara's letter *Love, Shadow*, she slipped the letter into a separate envelope from Tony's.

The next morning, after calling Baxter to tell him she was on her way, Shadow went to the kitchen where Mrs. Shevchuk was baking to tell her that she'd be back by eight that night, after she'd put the horses inside the barn. She handed Shadow a packed lunch, which Shadow knew would contain two peanut butter and jam sandwiches, juice, milk, diced carrots and apples, and a little box of raisins. Shadow smiled, then hugged and thanked her, knowing there would be stew on the stove and fresh-baked bread for her when she returned back home.

She stopped at the mailbox on her way to the farm. First, she dropped in a letter she'd written to Peter. Then, after anxiously shuffling the other two letters back and forth, she scrunched up her eyes, clenched her teeth, and pushed them through the slot as well, sighing with deep relief when it was done. "Let the chips fall as they may," she whispered to herself. It had been a difficult decision to write and send the letters to Tony and Barbara, but as she continued walking to the farm, she felt a weight had been lifted from her back, as though she'd spent her life carrying a heavy burden and now it was gone.

She arrived at the farm to find Baxter outside, waiting for her beside his newly waxed yellow car.

Racing Shadows

Instead of his normal sweaters and riding breeches, he had on a russet leather coat and matching pants, and a thick gold chain around his neck. She had to try and hide her amusement.

"Hullooo," he said, making the very word ooze sympathy. "What a nasty thing to happen to you yesterday. You must have been horrified, especially with a bun in the oven. You know, I'm so afraid of vicious dogs." Then he gasped as though a thought had hit him. "What if that monster got into our pasture or corrals! Could you imagine? I can't think what I'd do!" Then he stood there wringing his hands and reminding her of a giant fly.

Shadow regretted mentioning the dog incident when she'd spoken to him on the phone earlier. She shook her head. "Don't worry! The beach where it happened was miles away," she assured him. "And the owner of the dog had the animal under complete control. Anyway, I imagine the horses could make short work of a dog if they tried."

"Maybe if they got together and attacked it. But they'd likely panic instead and run through a fence or something awful. And you? Are you sure you weren't bitten?" he asked, looking her up and down. "They usually grab a leg or—"

"He didn't bite me," Shadow insisted. "Just growled a little. I'm perfectly fine."

Baxter stepped toward her and, making soothing noises, patted her back. "And in your condition too! You know there's the superstition that if a pregnant woman is frightened by a bear or—" He clamped both hands over his mouth as though realizing what he'd been about to say.

"I'm good," she assured him. "No harm. No foul. Where are you off to now, anyway?"

"Well, I won't go at all if you don't feel up to being alone," he said dramatically.

She smiled at him. "Don't worry. Looking after the horses can take my mind off of anything. Honest."

"Well..." he said, "if you insist. I planned a little shopping across the river for this afternoon and after that I have an engagement for the evening, dinner and the theater with a friend." He lifted his eyebrows at the word, "friend."

"Sounds fun."

"I'm hoping it will be. I should be home around midnight."

"I'll be back tomorrow morning," she said slowly. "You know Billie wants someone here overnight. If you can't be back, you should let me know."

"Oh, we'll be back, all right. My friend wants to see the place."

She cleared her throat. "Have you known this friend long?"

He lifted his chin, seemingly miffed at the question. "Long enough," he said as he got into his car and slammed the door.

She opened her mouth to say something, and then shut it. He was annoyed with her question, but he'd get over it. She was only trying to avoid what had happened

Racing Shadows

last week, when he'd come back from an "engagement" two hours late, in hysterics over a violent quarrel. She'd had to tell him she was calling an ambulance before he calmed down and made himself a cup of tea.

"Have a good night," she called after him as she waved goodbye.

When she walked into the barn, she could see that all of the stalls had been done and the track raked clean and smooth since the horses had been turned out. There was nothing much for her to do right then but clean some tack and keep an eye on the horses.

Hesitating at the tack room door, she thought about Peter's letter. He had so much more faith in her than she had in herself. She told herself that if she didn't start today, she never would.

Picking up the saddle, which was far heavier than it looked, she carried it over to Copper's stall, then returned to the tack room for the bridle and saddle pad. When she'd put down those too, she grabbed a halter and shank and slipped out the back door. She called Copper who was nosing some hay across the corral. The filly's head swept up in an arc as she spotted Shadow. Then she began to amble over. Before the gleaming chestnut could reach Shadow, a dark mare rushed between them, pinning back her ears and pointing her rump at Copper's approach.

"Go!" Shadow yelled at her. "Scram!" She tried to shove the horse away, but all that moved was her neck. Then the horse began to push back and Shadow doubled the leather shank and slapped her chest smartly until she got the picture and took off, buck-squealing across the corral.

"C'mere, Copper," she said. "Don't mind that grouch. Come to Shadow." The filly walked up and Shadow slipped on her halter, snapping the shank to it. After patting her, she led the filly back into the barn. Once the horse was in cross ties, Shadow showed her the saddle and pad. They were brand new without any smell of horse on them. Copper sniffed them without showing any fear. But when Shadow tried to put the pad on her back, she sidled away. "Don't be silly now," Shadow said softly. "It's a saddle, just like the ones you used to wear at the track. It goes on your back. So I can ride you."

Eventually, the filly stopped dancing about and Shadow managed to saddle and bridle her. Then she led her once around the track that circled the stalls. "Whoa!" she commanded when they'd reached Copper's stall again. Once the filly stood stock still, Shadow placed herself at the filly's left shoulder facing her tail.

With one hand holding the reins and grasping the saddle horn, Shadow raised her foot toward the stirrup … and wished she'd tried riding her three weeks ago when she was three weeks less pregnant. She dragged over a mounting block and tried again, the whole while repeating the words that Abby had told her before she left for Birchthorn. "It's impossible to fall out of a western saddle, impossible to fall out of a western saddle...."

Racing Shadows

Now able to reach the stirrup, Shadow mounted and found herself sitting on Copper's back. It had been incredibly easy! Shadow urged the filly forward with a cluck and squeeze of her legs. As the horse walked around the in-barn track, carrying Shadow, moving beneath her, it felt as though she and Shadow were one with each other. The horse's walk was as smooth as water, until she sped up to the trot. "Whoa!" Shadow said, about to rein the filly back when the horse instantly slowed back to the walk. One of her ears turned back to Shadow, as though listening.

Without knowing exactly what she was doing, her only lesson having been on the amusement park pony, she rode the filly out through the barn door, guiding her at a walk past the corrals and pasture to the empty field Peter had shown her.

By the time they arrived at the grassy field, Shadow felt very comfortable, almost as though she'd been born on a horse. Before she could lose her nerve, she picked up the reins and squeezed Copper's body firmly with her legs. Copper moved out at the trot. When Shadow squeezed again, the filly picked up a canter. Another squeeze and Copper surged forward at a gallop. The wind blowing in her face, Shadow clung to the filly's mane as they flew over the ground. When they approached a large pile of logs, Shadow feared Copper might leap them, but before reaching them, Shadow pulled on her left rein. They veered off to the left, Shadow now sitting back and deep into the saddle as though she were a part of it, a part of Copper. "Go,

Copper," Shadow urged with her legs and voice and they raced on round the huge meadow with such passion, such ecstasy, that Shadow lost track of how long they'd been running.

Eventually, Shadow slowed the filly, first to a trot, and then a walk as she guided her to a brook. Stepping into the flowing water, the horse bent her long neck down and thrust her muzzle into the stream. After sliding off of her back, Shadow crouched by Copper's left front leg and lifted the cold liquid in cupped hands to her face. She drank until she'd slaked her thirst.

As horse and rider ambled back to the barn, both of them cooling out, Shadow stopped Copper now and again at patches of tender grasses or clover. As the filly ate, Shadow marveled at what she had just done—the miracle of it. Copper was Peter's horse, and the experience of the ride was like a gift from him to her. One she'd never forget.

But most surprising of all, she felt that now, after she'd succeeded at this, she could literally do anything.

When she put away Copper's tack, groomed her, and returned her to her corral, Shadow climbed onto a wooden rail and watched the horses. Some of the leaves on nearby poplars had turned bright yellow and, early that morning when she'd looked out her window, she'd seen a trace of white glimmering from the barn roofs. She hugged herself—winter was coming.

To her left, a flurry sprang up in one corner, one horse kicking at another. Then they separated, running in opposite directions. A few seconds later, they came

Racing Shadows

back together and simultaneously scratched each other's backs with their teeth, as though nothing averse had happened between them. Copper grazed next to a yearling filly, the two of them ignoring the hay and sticking their heads through the fence rails to crop grass from the neighboring field. Shadow felt at peace as she watched the horses, their graceful movements, their colors and forms.

Slipping off the rail, she walked to the center of the corral and lay down among the horses. She listened to and felt them, their life and energy and souls. Soon, her thoughts strayed to her baby. Although she was determined to keep and raise it, she still harbored doubts. Closing her eyes, she re-lived the ride on Copper. Then thought about the track and the horses and Peter and how hard it would be to stay away from all of that because she was home with a baby.

"How will I do it?" she asked aloud. "How?"

"The same way you just learned to ride," she heard Peter's voice say as if he were right beside her.

She grinned. *Yes! The baby and I will be just fine!* With a feeling of new confidence, she climbed to her feet and filled the horses' grain bins, then opened the stall, barn, and corral doors wide. Although Baxter said it would be impossible, the horses did exactly as she'd taught them: They filed calmly, one by one, each into their own stall.

CHAPTER 19

If I wasn't positive I wanted to meet Marjorie, I'd never have called her, Shadow assured herself.

Marjorie had sounded friendly on the phone when Shadow rang her an hour earlier. If she was angry about Peter and Shadow's relationship, she wasn't letting it show. But Shadow still felt a little guilty. She felt as though Marjorie ought to hate her. Almost as if when she arrived at Marjorie's, she'd find her hiding behind the door with an axe in her hand. Ready to chop off Shadow's toes?

Very funny, she told herself with a frown.

Still, her apprehension was real—but obviously not as strong as her curiosity. In the month and a half since Shadow had met Marjorie on the beach, she'd yearned more and more to speak with her, discover just who she really was: the formless dwarf in the dark hooded coat on the lakeshore. She wanted to discover exactly what the woman and Peter meant to each other. She knew she probably shouldn't, but she couldn't help herself.

Although Shadow had invited Marjorie out for coffee in a downtown shop, she had explained that it

Racing Shadows

would be easier for her if Shadow came to her home. So Shadow agreed.

Shadow took her time getting ready. She decided to wear a dress. The closest thing to a dress that she had here, of course, was the white knit tunic and skirt she'd worn the day Copper had raced and she and Peter had had their "date." Hesitantly, she studied herself in the mirrored tile at the end of her room as she began changing her clothes. She didn't like what she saw in the mirror: her belly huge and taut as a drum, the skin stretched tight against the bulk of the child, her breasts heavy, so full that she'd had to start wearing a bra. She looked away, pulling on her skirt and tunic quickly.

Tony had succeeded in turning her into a woman, as he'd said he would.

She lifted the hem of her tunic and moved closer to the mirror, then stood still as a marble statue, waiting until finally, the baby moved, and she caught it in the mirror—the ripple beneath her very flesh. She shivered, then chided herself for being frightened. The books she'd read on the subject of pregnancy and childbirth said that it was normal for pregnant women to be afraid of the upcoming birth. It wasn't a bad thing or an ominous sign of any type. Shadow tried to believe them.

She was pleased that her outfit still fit her. Then she brushed her hair, knotting it at the nape of her neck, applied a slice of coral lipstick across her mouth, and was ready. For what? *To face the enemy? To meet with her competition?*

Mrs. Shevchuk had been sitting in the living room, waiting. In the early afternoons she'd often sit there, looking into the backyard. Dreaming? Seeing, once again, her children at play? Watching winter close over the world? Shadow didn't know. It was none of her business. One day, if she lived to that age, she'd find out for herself.

Last weekend, some of Mrs. Shevchuk's children and their families had come to visit. It had been an uproar and tumult. Fortunately, Shadow had been able to get away to the farm to work and ride Copper. When she came back Sunday night, all was well, but Mrs. Shevchuk had been tired ever since, not yet recovered from the visit, like a child whose party has been too exciting.

She touched the older woman's shoulder. "Shall I call the cab now?" She wondered if she really should take her along, but this was Mrs. Shevchuk's day to go out, so…. Could Marjorie secretly be angry? She'd sounded fine on the phone. Well, she'd hardly make a scene in front of an elderly lady. Then it struck Shadow—was she subconsciously taking Mrs. Shevchuk as a portable buffer zone?

"Yes, go ahead," Mrs. Shevchuk said. "I'm ready."

During the drive, Mrs. Shevchuk peered out the window and told Shadow how the countryside had changed over the years, what had once been here and once been there. Shadow listened with interest, trying to picture it. After following a narrow, winding road, the

Racing Shadows

cab drove them past hedged and gated yards, and finally arrived at a sign that said, "*Sand Castles.*" The driver left the cab, pressed a buzzer on one of the concrete pillars flanking either side of a gate, and it opened. They drove toward the house, and even from the back, Shadow could tell that it was the one she'd seen from the beach, the one she'd yearned to own.

"No," Shadow said to the driver. "Not the main house. We're looking for a small cottage on the grounds." Shadow looked around, seeing nothing. The driver got out of the cab and stood on tiptoes beside it. Then he said something Shadow didn't quite catch, got back into the cab and swung it around, coasting to the end of an asphalt driveway and stopping.

"Afraid you'll have to walk the rest of the way," he said.

They got out of the cab and Shadow paid him, telling him she'd call him when they were ready to leave. When she turned around, Mrs. Shevchuk was already partway down a paving-stone path to what looked like a storybook cottage—pale blue in color with pink-and-white striped awnings. Shadow jogged to catch up. As they walked the rest of the way together, Shadow glanced around nervously for the dog.

Shadow knocked, waiting anxiously for someone to answer the door. As the seconds spun past, her apprehension grew. She glanced at Mrs. Shevchuk, who smiled at her.

"Nibble nibble little mouse, who is nibbling at my house?" the older woman whispered and began to laugh.

Right, Shadow thought, remembering the witch who'd captured Hansel and Gretel. She tried to laugh along, but couldn't. That fairy tale had always scared her.

Then the door opened slowly, just a crack at first. Shadow heard someone speaking, but couldn't make out the words. Was it a chant, a curse?

The door opened another inch. "I'm sorry," someone said. "I can't get this silly cat... There! Got you!"

Then the door opened wide to reveal a little woman in a blue dress—much less sinister than the hunched form in the dark coat Shadow had met at the beach. Shadow relaxed a little.

"Come in," Marjorie said. "Welcome."

Shadow stepped across the threshold into the house, but Mrs. Shevchuk stood rooted where she was. "Never saw like that," she said in an awed tone.

"What?" Shadow asked, her heart jumping to her throat.

"Eyes of cat. Look. White!"

Resting against the shimmery blue brocade of Marjorie's bosom, was a sleek black cat with white eyes. She chuckled. "Well, he doesn't see so good. But isn't he pretty?"

Shadow shuddered. Briefly she felt the impulse to grab Mrs. Shevchuk and run.

Racing Shadows

After introductions, their hostess turned and led them down a hall. She walked very slowly and, from Shadow's position above her, she could see that the top of her head was bald, hair from behind her left ear combed up and over the slightly peaked dome of her skull. The rest of her hair rested in a curly brown nest on top of the slight hunch on her back.

"Please have a seat in there and I'll bring in your tea." She waved her arm toward a doorway and walked ahead, farther down the hall.

At the room's entrance, Shadow stopped short. From where she stood, she could see dozens of photographs ... almost all of Peter. Shadow began to tremble, feeling like one of those hard brown seed pods on a late summer's hedge—at the instant the pod is ready to burst. She crossed the room and gingerly sat on a blue velvet sofa. On the table at her elbow rested a framed photograph. She picked it up hesitantly, then cradled it in her lap.

From the photo, Peter smiled up at her. He was standing in front of the house they were in right now. He wore a grey-striped, belted jacket. A coiled rope was slung over his left shoulder, and his other hand was caught by its thumb in the jacket's belt. On his head was his cap; on his feet, hiking shoes. The many thick veins on his hands stood out clearly.

First, the recognition, the memory, made her heart race, but then the idea of Peter's image trapped here in Marjorie's house for her to view over and over again, hit her like a physical blow.

Her voice wavering slightly, she said, "This is Peter, from the race track." She handed the framed photo to Mrs. Shevchuk, who was now seated beside her.

Taking it, she nodded. "A nice boy," she said, then looked around the room. "Nice boy—nice room."

But Shadow wasn't looking at the room. She stared at the coffee table in front of her. On it rested a travel magazine, a writing tablet ... and an envelope addressed to Miss Marjorie Hipsley. In the upper left corner of it sat Peter's return address. She didn't understand why her heart suddenly plummeted. She knew Peter wrote to Marjorie, she knew he even came to visit her during the winter.

Taking the photo from Mrs. Shevchuk, Shadow set it back on the side table, then picked up the travel magazine, opening it and pointing out some things to Mrs. Shevchuk, making conversation as they waited.

"Are you sure I can't help you with something?" she called to their hostess when it seemed as though she'd never return.

"Yes, you can. I'm ready now. You can help me carry."

Shadow helped Marjorie transfer an assortment of sweets and savories to the coffee table, as well as tea in a silver service.

"You have beautiful house," Mrs. Shevchuk said. "You a piano teacher? Or maybe artist?" she asked, nodding toward a small room off to the right that was furnished with a piano, chairs, and a bookcase. Sitting

Racing Shadows

on a wooden easel was a partially-completed painting of Peter.

The white-eyed cat walked around Marjorie's feet, which dangled from her chair where she sat across from them. The cat strolled back and forth, in and out, rubbing against her bowed legs and the heavy black shoes she wore.

"No, I play and paint only for pleasure. Fortunately, I don't have to do anything to earn my living."

"Do you look after the big house during the winter?" Shadow asked.

"No," she said. "I could hardly do that, could I? No, a hired man and his wife live there as caretakers. When summer comes closer, they'll doubtless begin to clean things up around here." She chuckled. "No. My relatives allow me to live here in this cottage. For them, it's a more palatable alternative than having me join them across the river. And I prefer it myself." She smiled, her face ruddy and broad. She caught Shadow staring and raised her thick, dark eyebrows, as if amused.

The situation reminded Shadow of something Paul had told her: how every fall starving dogs roamed the streets of the town. Dogs that the American summer residents had abandoned, unwilling to take them back to their U.S. homes, leaving them here to fend for themselves. She realized she was blushing in shame for Marjorie's relatives, whoever they were.

"You must enjoy living here," Shadow commented, trying to sound cheerful, "so close to the lake."

"Yes, I love it. I especially love when it storms." She smiled.

"Your big dog," Mrs. Shevchuk suddenly asked. "Where you keep him?"

"Oh, he's in and out all day long. Out right now—in the woods or down at the beach. He avoids strangers. It's almost as though he knows, ahead of time, when someone is coming to see me."

Mrs. Shevchuk nodded. "I have dog too. Shadow takes him out for walk. I'm too old walk with dog now."

"Fortunately, Darkness can go outside whenever he likes."

Mrs. Shevchuk nodded. "No much traffic."

"He stays off the roads. So yes, perfectly safe."

"Does he ever bite?" Shadow asked, not meaning to be rude, but just wondering how close she came.

Marjorie shook her head. "No. And he only growled at you because I'd come up behind you. Silly boy thought he needed to protect me. I wonder where he got that idea?" she mused, looking at Shadow intently.

Shadow gasped, but inwardly.

"After all," Marjorie continued, "you've got to allow him that—I am his best friend." At this, she laughed out loud.

When Shadow looked at her blankly, she said, "Dog is man's best friend; so woman is dog's best friend. The balance makes sense, doesn't it?"

Without waiting for an answer, she hopped down off her chair and shuffled across the plush blue carpet

Racing Shadows

toward Shadow. Shadow felt gentle fingers grazing her cheek, tracing her hair where it was pulled back behind her ears. Although at the beach, she'd have been horrified if Marjorie had reached out to her, she didn't recoil from her touch now. Instead, she smiled.

"I'm sorry Darkness frightened you," the woman said. "I'm sorry *I* frightened you." And then she just stared at Shadow, her lips pale in her ruddy face. Finally turning away, she lifted a framed photograph from the shelf of a cabinet and placed it into Shadow's hands.

It was a black-and-white portrait of a formally dressed man and woman with a curly-haired little girl in a white dress seated between them. After examining it for a few seconds, Shadow said, "Cute. Who are they?"

"My father, my mother, and me. When I was three. Wasn't I pretty? They loved me then, you know."

"I'm sure they did, and do still," Shadow said.

Mrs. Shevchuk cleared her throat. "Shadow grew up foster care. Doesn't know real mother, father."

Shadow held her breath, waiting for Marjorie to say, *"Yes, Peter told me."*

"How unlucky for you," she said instead, turning toward Shadow.

"You could call it that," Shadow replied.

"Do you ever want to know who your parents are?" Marjorie asked bluntly, then added, "I've read that a lot of adopted and foster children do."

Shadow shrugged. "A little." Then hesitated. "I always ... well, I'd like to ask my mother why she gave me up. And I'd like to know what she looked like and

... I must've had a father too...." Her words trailed off. She couldn't believe she'd said those words out loud— to a veritable stranger no less.

"You know," Marjorie said. "There are ways to find out these things. If you like, I could help you. I certainly have the time."

Shadow didn't reply, and the offer hung unacknowledged in the air. They ate the snacks ... sipped their tea. The house was set high enough that they could see a view of the lake through the big picture window, making it almost as though the lake was part of the very room, grey and so windswept you could almost hear the waves, feel the air wet with spray.

Every so often, the women's eyes seemed to meet.

"I'd be grateful if you would," Shadow said quietly, although several minutes had passed since Marjorie had spoken. Marjorie was the second person who had offered to help her find her real parents, although Billie had only offered to find her mother, who was on the Indian side. He hadn't said anything about helping locate her white father.

Marjorie nodded once and smiled. "Good."

Shadow leaned back against the cushions. She felt inexplicably light.

"When is the baby due?" Marjorie asked.

"Just under two months," Shadow replied.

She smiled. "Some say that a woman is at her most beautiful when she's pregnant."

Shadow looked at her, really looked at her—her twisted form, her misshapen head—remembered her

Racing Shadows

own nightmares of being an ugly creature with cloven hooves. *My dreams were of her; she is the personification of that fear,* Shadow realized.

"We have to go now," Shadow said in a rush. "We've been here too long. Thank you so much for the tea. And I'm sorry about—" She was afraid to finish.

"Sorry about what?" Marjorie asked gently.

"Sorry about Peter." There.

Marjorie shook her head. "There's no need. Honestly. You take care and call me again soon. Please."

Shadow stared at her. She wanted to say something kind, but couldn't think of anything and then wondered if Marjorie truly knew about Shadow and Peter, knew that she and Shadow were competing for his letters, his time … his *love?*

Shadow cleared her throat. "Yes, I'll call…" she began, but stopped because it felt dishonest.

"You look upset," Marjorie said. "Can I ask you a question?"

Shadow nodded, her jaw and stomach tightening.

"Do you love Peter?"

"Yes," she said without hesitation.

"Good," Marjorie replied. "So do I."

Shadow froze.

Marjorie chuckled. "But don't you worry, he's big enough for the both of us." Then she laughed out loud, and Mrs. Shevchuk laughed along with her, until the troubled frown melted from Shadow's face, turning into a smile.

IA Moore

A wind had blown up from the lake as Mrs. Shevchuk and Shadow walked away from the small house, their coats being blown against them, pressed to their bodies, the elderly woman's body now slack and resting, Shadow's filled with life and hope. As they got into the cab, Shadow turned back to wave to Marjorie, who was leaning against the doorframe in her bright blue dress, the black cat once again wrapped in her arms, its white eyes emptily staring. And from across the lawns, Darkness came galloping toward his mistress, as though he'd only been waiting for her visitors to leave.

Later that night, when Mrs. Shevchuk had gone to bed, Shadow walked down the long road leading to the farm. In the distance, she could hear the river, the sound of rushing water. In her mind, she listened to Peter's voice telling her the story about the Indian girl and the horses. She breathed in deeply. The air smelled of the coming winter, smelled of loss. Shivering, she pulled her jacket tighter around her. She was startled by a piercing cry, and great pale wings flashed across her path, brushing her eyes. *Winter owl*, she thought. And she wondered about the animals. When winter came, did they know there'd be a spring?

When she reached the farm, the light in Baxter's trailer window was still on, a square yellow glow. She decided to stop in because she'd promised to visit him, many times, and never had. Still, she was coming unannounced. Shouldn't she have called first? Before

Racing Shadows

she could chicken out, her knuckles rapped at his door. She knocked softly at first, then harder.

When the door opened, Baxter looked as if he had just woken up. "I'm sorry," Shadow said, "I saw the light...."

"Come in, come in," he said and she did.

He led her to the kitchen table and made them both coffee. Across the green Formica table top, they talked until midnight. About horses, about his family, about owls and lakes, and about everything else that came to mind.

Before she started home, she went out to the barn to see Copper and found her lying down in her stall. Crouching low, she threw her arms about the filly's neck and hugged her. "Everything will be okay," Shadow said. "Don't you worry, it will all be fine."

CHAPTER 20

Before leaving the house, Shadow climbed the stairs as quietly as she could to Abby's old room, pleased to find that the door wasn't locked. It opened silently when she turned the crystal glass knob. She crossed the wooden floor to the closet, where she could see a few clothes still hanging: winter things, heavy sweaters and jackets that Abby wouldn't need until spring, what with her exercising horses in Florida. Grasping the sleeve of a cardigan, she ran the soft fabric through her fingers.

Finally, she turned from the closet, walked to the dresser and carefully set down what she'd brought. Set down the gift she was offering in return for the pommel pad that Abby had given her. She ran her hand over the sleek marble, the strongly curved neck.

Reaching into her purse, she pulled out a piece of paper and a pen. On it she wrote: *"He flies without wings and conquers without sword. In the wind of his nostrils, remember me! —Shadow."*

Then she looked into the dresser mirror and saw her face, streaked with tears. *Yes, that's me,* she thought. *That's finally me.*

Racing Shadows

She watched out the window until the limousine pulled up into the yard and the dark-uniformed driver walked toward the house, then clomped up the front steps. She pushed her bag across the doorway to him. It was still dark outside. A light dusting of new-fallen snow covered everything. Halfway down the steps, she turned back at a noise to see that Squeaks had jumped up at the inside window of the front door. His nails clawed at the wood, and his nose bumped the window glass, as if he wanted to come with her.

"Stay home," Shadow mouthed, blew the dog a kiss, and climbed inside the limo.

When Shadow had received Barbara's letter, she'd been shocked, then saddened, and then, at last, relieved. The letter revealed that a month earlier, Tony had died at the end of a week-long diabetic coma.

This meant that, *if* she decided that she wanted to, she could go home safely, have the baby, then in a year or two, go on to college or university while living at home with Barbara. Barbara would tend her child as if it were her own. The past was gone. Tony was gone. And Barbara loved her.

Of course, Shadow hadn't made any firm decisions. Right now, she was just visiting Barbara to help comfort her in her time of mourning.

Shadow was the only passenger sitting in the back seat of the limo. There were two men in camel hair coats sitting in the front beside the driver. The heat didn't seem to reach to the back of the vehicle. She asked the driver to turn it up, then looked out the window, watching the headlights of the other cars and trucks hurtling toward, then past them in the dark. She thought about her old house in Edmonton, the warmth, the smells of cooking, and stopped herself from thinking about anything else, stopped her memories of the other things. When they passed St. Catharines, she was still cold, but before she could ask the driver to turn up the heat again, she dozed off. When she awoke, they were driving over the Burlington Skyway. Her feet were frozen; she couldn't feel her toes. "I need more heat back here," she said, her voice fuzzy in her ears.

"Sorry, it's on full blast."

One of the men turned to her. "You want to switch seats?" he offered. "It's plenty warm up here."

"No thanks," she replied as she huddled back into the corner of the seat, resting her head between the seat back and the side of the car. Closing her eyes, she breathed deeply and tried to ignore the cold.

Shadow is in a small room. She is sitting on a large, low table with a light shining in her face. She knows she's supposed to wait, so she does, but the waiting makes her nervous. Finally, a man walks into the room. Wearing a dark trench coat with a black fedora pulled low over his face, he approaches her. "It's your time," he says.

Slowly, he takes off his hat, and she recognizes him. Tony!

Racing Shadows

"You're supposed to be dead," she whispers.

He laughs. "Look at you!" he says.

Looking down at herself, she sees she's wearing a white gown, her belly like a mountain beneath it. She puts one hand to her middle and feels a pain begin, the thick muscle contracting.

Her breath comes in gulps. Tony comes even closer. "Calm down," he says. "It's important to stay calm. Your time is here." Then he puts a hand on each of her knees, and using great force, pries her legs apart. She screams in pain, but he doesn't stop. Then he plunges his hands into her birth canal, trying to reach her baby and pull it out.

"No," she screams. "You can't have my baby! Leave it alone."

"Oh, but I have permission."

Then he stops what he's doing, rubs his bloodied red hands together, and looks over his shoulder. She follows his gaze and, through a small window in the grey metal door, she sees Barbara's dark eyes watching them.

She struggles frantically, but he holds her down, this time plunging his hands even deeper until…

She woke up screaming. Concerned voices from the men in the front seat reminded her of where she was and she calmed down.

"I'm all right," she told them, still panting. "I'm all right. I fell asleep and … and had a nightmare."

IA Moore

The men chuckled as if relieved. "Oh, is that all? We thought you were going into labor. Whew, close call!" Then they fell back into conversation, leaving her on her own to try and slow her heart's mad beating.

Shadow was still shaking when half an hour later, she stepped through the sliding doors into the Toronto airport. Surrounding her was a confusing jumble of counters, signs, luggage carousels, and people; people rushing past, or in and out of doors, or standing beside carts piled to overflowing with suitcases and boxes.

Just when she thought she was going to be sick, she saw ... Peter, smiling at her.

She'd called him two days earlier when she received Barbara's letter with the airline ticket inside. Explained to Peter how Barbara had taken care of her for most of her life, had been a mother to her, how they'd loved one another, and how now that she was a widow and alone, Shadow had to go back home and comfort her. Peter hadn't tried to change her mind as she'd half expected him to. All he'd asked her was when she was leaving, what time, and from where.

Peter quickly walked over to her, silently taking her bag, and she walked beside him to a small restaurant inside the building. Once they were sitting down, she asked, "Have you come to see me off?"

He remained silent and just stared at her. She stared back, the familiarity of his face both warming her and filling her with regret at the same instant.

"Peter?"

Racing Shadows

"Do you know what you really want?" he asked. "Never mind what anyone else wants of you," he insisted. "Do you know what YOU want?"

She shook her head without saying a word.

"Please take off your coat," he said. "Stand up and let me see you."

Her coat slipped off of her shoulders onto the back of the chair. She got slowly to her feet, stepping out from behind the table to where he could see her. With both hands, she smoothed her loose-fitting shirt over the baby.

When she got up the courage to look at Peter, he was staring at her, all of her, every part in turn. She stepped closer to him, taking his hand, and slipped it under her shirt, onto her skin. At first, he held back, touching her so lightly that all she could feel was the scratchiness of his calloused skin, then he pressed more firmly, and the warmth of his hand travelled through her body.

"I won't let you go alone," he said, slipping from his chair to stand in front of her, his arms around her waist, head pillowed against her.

"Tell me that's all right," he whispered so low she could barely hear it. They stayed in an embrace for several minutes until he told her she should get off of her feet and sit.

"It's all right," she said as they moved apart from one another. "It's good."

When they were sitting again, he smiled and asked, "Tell me. Have you ridden her yet?"

She nodded. "Yes, thank you," she said. "It was beautiful."

"I told you, you could do it." He wiped a tear from her cheek.

Trying not to break down completely, she concentrated on the plate of yellow and orange Jell-O squares she'd ordered, jiggled them a little with her spoon.

"Want this?" she asked, scooping up the little white cone of whipped cream from the top of the dessert.

He opened his mouth. Carefully, she set it on his tongue and he closed his lips around the spoon.

She laughed.

"Practicing?" he asked.

"Oh, Peter—" she began, but didn't know how to finish, how to tell him she might be saying a permanent goodbye to him once they reached the Edmonton airport. That there was a chance that she'd never come back to Fort Eldon.

"Eat your Jell-O and then we'll get checked in and go to the boarding area," he said.

She didn't move, just sat where she was, all of her energy having seemed to seep down and drain out of her toes.

He waited.

Finally, she said, "I thought you'd try and convince me to stay. I thought you'd want that."

"It's not what I want, or Paul wants, or Billie wants or anybody else wants that's important here."

Racing Shadows

She put her hands over her face. "I just don't know what to do! Every choice seems wrong."

"You said that you were going home to someone who loves you. Are you sure?"

Even an hour ago, she would have answered, *Yes!* Now—after the dream of Barbara watching through the window as Tony tried to steal her unborn baby—she was uncertain. Still, there were things she had to find out, demons she had to confront. She wasn't going to be frightened away. Not anymore. "I guess that's what I have to find out."

He took her hands in his, squeezed them. "My brave Shadow!" he said.

Several hours later, Barbara met Shadow as she made her way to the luggage carousel at the Edmonton airport. Barbara pulled her into a hug. Shadow's body stiffened involuntarily beneath her coat. She hoped Barbara didn't notice. "Mom," she said.

"Welcome home, baby" Barbara crooned, and Shadow wondered once again how Barbara truly felt about Shadow carrying Tony's child, a child she'd been unable to bear him. Could she really still love her?

Barbara chattered on about unimportant things as they watched the luggage spin round. Shadow's bag glided by, but she pretended not to notice.

"Did you know?" Shadow finally asked, her voice seeming to speak of itself, against her will.

"Know what?" Barbara asked.

"Did you know, I asked you!" Shadow repeated loudly, grasping Barbara's shoulders. She needed to hear the truth from her lips. Her denials by letter weren't good enough.

Barbara shook her head, but then her face contorted and she began to cry.

Shadow reached into her pocket, grasping the medicine pouch that Billie had given her. Pressing it into Barbara's hand, she closed Barbara's fingers around it. "Tell me the truth, Mom. I need to know!"

Tears streaming, Barbara shook her head and looked past Shadow, her eyes desperate.

"Answer me!"

"Yes!" she yelled, so loudly that the flesh on her face quivered. Then she whispered harshly, "They'd have taken you away from me! Don't you understand?" Then she moaned out loud, a sound that seemed to issue from deep inside her. "Of course, I knew!" Again, she looked past Shadow to something behind.

Shadow turned quickly and saw a shape dodge past the edge of the nearest plate-glass door. A shape she recognized.

Whirling to face Barbara, she stared into her black eyes. "Tony's here, isn't he," she said. "Isn't he!" And suddenly, she saw Barbara in a way she'd never seen her before: weak, alone, and afraid.

Barbara dropped her eyes. "I *had* to lie to you to bring you back." Then she looked up again, a smile shining through her tears. "I lied for your own good."

"What!" Shadow was incredulous.

Racing Shadows

"The baby will stay with us, all of our family together. It's the right way. Just as a woman belongs to her husband, so the child belongs to its father!"

"No one belongs to anyone else!" Shadow said, her voice low and threatening. Grabbing the pouch out of Barbara's hand, she yelled, "Stay away from me!"

When she turned, Shadow saw Peter standing with two policemen near the doors.

"Outside!" Shadow yelled to them as she ran after Tony, racing out into the icy Edmonton air. When the officers ran past her, she stopped, knowing that as soon as they caught and brought Tony back, she would confront him. Then she'd testify against him in court, and once that was done, she would go back where she belonged, back to Peter and Copper, back to her real friends and her new life.

As Peter caught up to her and took her hand, she found that her heart wasn't filled with hatred for Tony anymore, but only with love for Peter: there wasn't room for anything else. She glowed within, as warm as the summer sun, realizing that Peter was the one who truly loved her, and she him, and that she would never leave him again.

ABOUT THE AUTHOR

I.A. Moore has worked and played with horses for many years. Her most recent passion is writing stories and books about them.

She has a Bachelor of Science Degree in Zoology and University-level training in Creative Writing and English. Her stories have been published in numerous magazines and broadcast on radio. She resides in Fort Erie, Ontario, Canada.

IA Moore

NOTE FROM THE AUTHOR

Thank you for reading this book. I hope you enjoyed it!

REVIEWS

If you enjoyed this book, please leave a review to help other readers to find it.

IA Moore

MORE BOOKS

Please visit my Amazon Page for updates. Also, check out my other books.

LIST OF BOOKS

A Pony for the Fair
Equine Elegance
Equine Grace
Hooves and Heartbeats
Racing Fever
Racing Hearts
Racing Shadows
Racing Trouble

Printed in Great Britain
by Amazon